KATE VENTER

Say it with Sugar

IN COLLABORATION WITH

CYNTHIA FLETCHER

AND

FRANCES BELL

MEREHURST

Published 1990 by Merehurst Limited,
Ferry House, 51/57 Lacy Road, Putney, London SW15 1PR.
By arrangement with Tafelberg Publishers Ltd
First edition 1990
Reprinted 1991, 1992 (twice), 1994

© Tafelberg Publishers Limited

ISBN 1 85391 148 8

Photography by Dick Bomford
Illustrations by Anne Westoby
Cover and typography by G&G Design
Set in 10 on 12 pt Plantin Monotype Lasercomp
Printed and bound by Toppan Printing Company (H.K.) Ltd,
Hong Kong

Contents

Acknowledgements

Our sincere thanks go to the following people:

☐ Irene Pienaar, Agata Pomario, Ina Goulden and Jackie Duncan who made all the tiny time-consuming flowers used for filling gaps.

☐ Henry Willis, who once again supplied us with the necessary cutters.

☐ Editor Madaleine du Plessis, who assisted us with the writing and translation of *Sugar art* and *Sugar decorating*, and who was never satisfied until she thought every detail would be clear to novices.

☐ Our families for their faith in our abilities, their tolerance and loving support.

☐ Our students and friends for their encouragement and support.

☐ The publishers who made our third book a reality and our editor, Dalene Müller.

☐ Our Creator, who bestowed us with our talents and gave us strength throughout.

The authors

Special techniques and recipes

In *Sugar art* and *Sugar decorating*, to which this book is a sequel, the tried and tested recipes are given for fruit cakes, fondant, royal icing, flood icing and modelling paste. It would be superfluous to repeat the recipes here, particularly as cake decorators generally have their own recipes or use commercially available mixtures. The techniques of bas-relief work, silhouette work, cocoa painting, mould making, figure modelling and dressing figures need, however, to be dealt with in detail.

Bas-relief work

This is a technique in which figures are moulded out of flower paste so that, when they are placed on a cake, they stand out slightly from the background. It can best be illustrated by means of an example (*plate 1*).

☐ Make a photocopy of the pattern (*diagram 33*) and place it on a board. Cover it with plastic and secure it so that it cannot move.

☐ Using the pattern as guideline, mould the flowers and leaves freehand, or use cutters of a suitable size. Set aside to dry.

☐ Next, mould the central figure (the mouse). Start with that part of his body furthest away from you, i.e. the part of the foot visible under the stalk. Mould it freehand and place it in position. Shape the leg of this foot.

☐ Add the trousers turn-up and tuck it under the leg with a scalpel or similar tool to create the impression that it goes right around.

☐ Mould the hand behind the stalk and place it in position. Make the arm.

☐ Make the flower stalk and arrange it over the hand and foot.

☐ Mould and position the tail, second foot and trousers.

☐ Add the second turn-up, tucking it under as well.

☐ Shape the body.

☐ Roll out a piece of flower paste and cut out the jacket according to the pattern. Drape it over the body.

☐ Make and position the ear furthest away from

Plate 1
Plaque in bas-relief.
(See *diagram 33* for pattern.)

you, then shape the head and add the second ear.

☐ Make the collar and place it in position.

☐ Shape the second hand and arm.

☐ Paint facial and other details on the figure.

☐ Set aside to dry.

☐ Make other components of the picture.

☐ Place the photocopy of your pattern on a plaque or cake and prick out the pattern outlines with a pin or similar sharp instrument.

☐ Paint the background and all those features not made of flower paste.

☐ Attach the moulded parts with royal icing, starting at the focal point.

☐ Finish off the border with roping, lace or whatever you choose.

Silhouette work
(after the technique developed by Denise Fryer)

Silhouette work (*plate 2*) is the shadowlike representation of the shape of something. It is filled in with a solid colour (usually black) and resembles the silhouettes, cut from paper, that were so popular last century.

☐ Dilute a little *silhouette paste* with just enough water to obtain an ink consistency.

☐ Using this ink and a mapping pen, trace the design onto tracing paper (*diagram 28*). Allow to dry completely.

☐ Place the tracing, ink side down, on the cake or plaque and secure it with pins.

☐ Gently rub over the back of the design with a pencil to get a transfer of it on the cake or plaque.

☐ For the actual painting, place a heap of about 10 ml (2 t) sifted icing sugar, a blob of black paste colouring and 2,5 ml (½ t) egg white in a circle around the hollow of a saucer. Draw the three ingredients to the centre with a thick brush (No. 2) and blend them to form a smooth, shiny "paint". (*Note:* Mix only a few drops at a time, taking care not to add too much or too little sugar. Too much sugar will result in a grainy texture, while too little will cause the "paint" not to adhere properly.)

☐ Colour in the picture and set it aside to dry, then add highlights with sparingly used tube work. (*Alternative:* Leave certain lines or areas unpainted to give life and dimension to the silhouette.)

Cocoa painting

This technique is very similar to watercolour painting, and is done with a mixture of cocoa powder and cocoa butter, or coconut oil, or white vegetable fat – never use any other colourings, as you then deviate from what the name implies. Cocoa painting can be done on rolled-out marzipan or plastic icing but not on pastillage, which is too porous. It is usually finished off with a frame or a border (*plates 39* and *45*).

☐ *Transferring a design onto a cake or plaque:* Trace off the pattern (see *diagram 29* for an example), turn the paper over and copy the outlines in pencil. Place the traced-off pattern, right side up, on the surface of the cake or plaque (it should be completely dry) and go over the outlines again to get a transfer.

☐ *Mixing the cocoa paint:* Melt a little cocoa butter or fat in three separate containers and add enough cocoa powder to each to obtain three tints: dark brown, medium brown and light brown. Keep them liquid on a hot tray or hotplate set to a very low temperature or over hot water.

☐ *Painting technique:* Work from top to bottom. Copy the outlines of the first section with a fine brush and the darkest tint, then shade it in with all three tints to give depth to the drawing. Leave unpainted areas where you wish to add highlights. Repeat the procedure until the picture is complete, then study it critically and add a few finishing touches, or scrape off colouring to add more highlights where necessary. (*Hint:* If your design is a copy of a colour picture, keep the original handy to serve as guide for highlighting and shading.)

Moulds

Either use commercial moulds, or make your own using plaster of Paris, quick-setting putty or ceramic clay. Taking a doll as an example, this is how you go about it:

Plaster of Paris mould
☐ Grease the doll well with vegetable fat or petroleum jelly and place it in a hollow container, securing it in position with wonder putty.

☐ Fill the container with pottery clay reaching halfway up the body of the doll.

☐ Mix some plaster of Paris according to the manufacturer's instructions and pour it slowly over the doll, covering it completely. Tap the container lightly on the table to remove all air bubbles.

Plate 2
Silhouette work on a background applied with blue aerosol food colouring (made and distributed by Denise Fryer) finishes the sides of this octagonal cake for the coming-of-age of a diver. (See *diagram 28* for patterns.) The figure was made according to the Mexican method, while the aqualung, goggles and shells were moulded free-hand. (*Note:* If preferred, the background colouring may be sprayed on with an airbrush.)

☐ Set aside for at least 30 minutes to dry, then unmould.
☐ To make a mould for the other half of the doll, repeat procedure, but place the doll upside down.

Note
☐ Remove the doll's arms and legs before making the moulds, as they are later shaped freehand to comply with the requirements of the design.
☐ This method is suitable only for figures with a uniform shape.

Ceramic clay or putty mould
☐ Rub your hands with vegetable fat or petroleum jelly and knead the clay or putty well, until it is soft and pliable.
☐ Press it over one half of the doll, making sure that all hollows are filled, otherwise certain features will be indistinct.
☐ Leave on the doll until almost set, then remove very carefully, taking care that the mould does not lose its shape. Set aside to harden completely.
☐ Repeat procedure for other half of doll.

Recipes

Pastillage 1
15 ml (1 T) gelatine (10 g)
60 ml (¼ c) cold water
10 ml (2 t) liquid glucose
5 ml (1 t) cream of tartar, dissolved in 10 ml (2 t) cold water
500-750 ml (2-3 c) sifted icing sugar (250-380 g)
250 ml (1 c) cornflour (120 g)

Soak the gelatine in the cold water, then melt it over hot water.
    Add the glucose and cream of tartar to the solution, and stir until well mixed.
    Place half the icing sugar and all the cornflour in a large mixing bowl. Add liquid and beat until mixture becomes sticky.
    Pour into an airtight container and store in the refrigerator.
    When needed, take the required quantity of mixture and add enough of the remaining sifted icing sugar to it to form a paste that does not stick to your hands.

Pastillage 2
2,5 ml (½ t) gum tragacanth
125 ml (4 heaped T) royal icing
sifted icing sugar

Stir the gum tragacanth into the icing, cover it with a damp cloth and, to prevent drying out, place it bowl and all in a plastic bag. Leave to stand overnight.
    Mix well the following day, adding enough sifted icing sugar to make the pastillage very stiff. Knead well until smooth.
    Use the paste for modelling animals, figures, bells, and suchlike.

Pollen
semolina *or* cornflour *or* gelatine powder
yellow colouring powder

Mix small amounts of the two ingredients together, using as much powdered colouring as will give you the tint of yellow you require.

Modelling figures and dressing them

☐ Mould the head, pressing the clay firmly into the mould. Insert a toothpick through the neck into the head, leaving about 20 mm protruding. Set aside to dry.

☐ Mould a piece of flower paste into the shape of a pear (*diagram 1A*). Cut a slit into the pointed end, measuring one and a half times the length of the head (*diagram 1B*). Shape the legs, with the knees about one head's length from the bottom. Shape the feet.

☐ Push a piece of wire horizontally through the top of the body, leaving about 3 mm protruding on either side (*diagram 1C*).

☐ Shape the body into the desired posture by bending the knees, torso, etc. If you wish it to stand upright, insert short lengths of florist's wire into the legs, leaving about 10 mm to 20 mm protruding at the feet.

☐ Affix the head to the body and set aside to dry.

☐ To make the arms, roll a small piece of paste into a sausage and flatten one end into a paddle shape (*diagram 1D*). The paddle (= the hand) should be the same length as the face from the chin to the middle of the forehead.

☐ Cut a wedge from the paddle to form the thumb (*diagram 1E*), then cut out the other four fingers and roll them all into shape *(diagram 1F)*. With the back of a scalpel or knife, make an incision in the hand just below the fingers and fold them inwards so they look natural and relaxed. Alternatively, if required, shape the hand and fingers as if holding something, a bunch of flowers, for example.

☐ Shape the forearm and upper arm, with the elbow about one head's length away from the hand (*diagram 1E*). (*Note:* The whole arm measures about one and a half times the length of the head. Be sure to make a pair of arms, one left and one right arm.)

☐ Bend the arms as desired and make a hole in each at shoulder level with the wires protruding from the body. Allow to dry separately on a piece of sponge or wadding.

☐ When everything is completely dry, the figure can be dressed. For a little girl, make the back of the dress first. Roll out a piece of flower paste very thinly and cut it out, using *diagram 2A* as a pattern. Brush a 2 mm-wide strip of egg white along the seam edges, taking care not to get any egg white on the right side of the paste. Attach the paste to the back of the body, draping it as desired. Repeat procedure for the front, placing the seam edges over those of the back. Smooth the seams with the heel of a veining tool to make them as inconspicuous as possible.

☐ Cut a sleeve out of a piece of rolled-out flower paste (*diagram 2B*) and brush a 2 mm-wide strip of egg white along the inside edge of the back part of the seam. Attach the sleeve to an arm and fold it over, joining and smoothing the front and back seam parts as described in the previous step. Dress the other arm in the same way.

☐ Brush a small ball of flower paste liberally with egg white and press it over the protruding wire at the right shoulder. Apply some egg white to the right arm around the hole and attach the arm to the body, forming a "mortise and tenon joint". Brush the inside edge of the sleeve head

Diagram 1
Modelling the legs and arms of a figure.

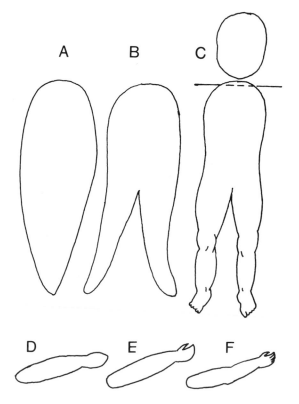

with egg white and join it very neatly to the arm-hole of the dress. Repeat procedure for left arm, and set aside to dry.

☐ Cut out the collar (*diagram 2C*) and attach it with egg white.

☐ To dress a little boy, cut out two of the trousers pattern (*diagram 3A*), one for the left and one for the right leg. First attach one of the legs, joining and smoothing the seam as described for the sleeves, then apply egg white to the centre front, centre back and waist of the body, and attach the top part of the pants. Repeat procedure for the other leg.

☐ Cut out two of the shirt pattern (*diagram 3B*). Attach first the back and then the front. Cut out and attach the collar (*diagram 3C*). Cut out and attach two sleeves (*diagram 2B*).

Note

These patterns are very simple and may either be elaborated upon or trimmed with pockets, cuffs, ties, etc.

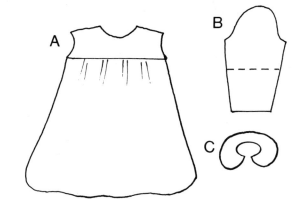

Diagram 2
Dress, collar and sleeve pattern for a girl.

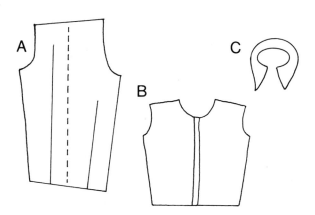

Diagram 3
Front/back, collar and sleeve pattern for a boy.

Flowers

Purple wreath *(Petrea kohautiana)*

The petrea blooms profusely and has lovely sprays of violet-blue flowers up to 30 cm in length *(plate 3)*. The sepals are lighter in colour than the corolla, which fades to greyish-brown and falls out before the flower dies.

Bud
☐ Bend a small hook at one end of a piece of 32-gauge wire *(diagram 4A)*. Mould a 5-mm ball of violet-blue flower paste around it in the form of a teardrop, about 10 mm long and 3 mm in diameter, at the rounded tip *(diagrams 4B and 4C)*.
☐ Make five evenly spaced incisions halfway down the teardrop *(diagram 4D)*.

Small flowers at top of spray
☐ Make as for bud, then cut the incisions open and separate the petals. *(Alternative:* Mould some flower paste into the shape of a hat with a pointed crown and wide brim, cut it out with a template and insert a hooked wire into it – see *diagrams 4E* and *5A.)*
☐ Thin out and widen the petals with an anger or small ball tool.
☐ Secure a 1-mm ball of flower paste at the heart of the flower with egg white to represent the beginning of the corolla.

Medium-sized flowers
☐ Follow alternative method for making small flowers, but use a larger template *(diagrams 4F and 5B)*.
☐ Widen and thin out the petals, then hollow out the tube of the flower with a toothpick or the point of a 3-mm knitting needle *(diagram 4G)*. Bend back the petals to prevent their spreading out like fingers.
☐ Make a bigger bud for the corolla and place it in the centre, securing it with egg white *(diagram 4H)*.

Large flowers with corolla
☐ Follow first step for making medium-sized flowers, but use a larger template *(diagram 5C)*.
☐ Roll out a darker shade of flower paste thinly and cut it out with the template for the corolla *(diagram 5E)*.
☐ Thin it out with a ball tool and secure it with egg white in the middle of the petals *(diagram 4I)*.
☐ Hollow out the tube of the flower with the point of your anger tool, pressing it right through the centre of the corolla.
☐ Paint the heart an even darker shade of purple, but leave the throat white.

Old flowers without corolla
Repeat the above procedure, but use a larger template *(diagram 5D)* and leave out the corolla (it falls out as the flower gets older).

Plate 3
A spray of petreas and chrysanthemums.

12

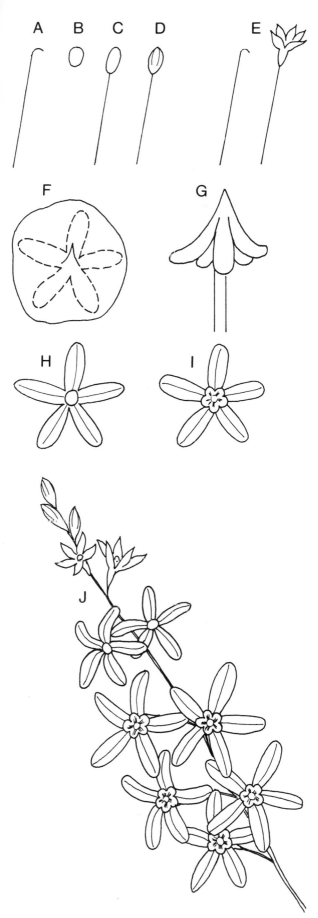

Assembling a spray

☐ Cover a piece of 28-gauge wire with white florist's tape and tape three buds to the tip.

☐ Tape two or three small flowers just below the buds, about 10 mm apart (the tip of the petals should reach about halfway up the flower above it).

☐ Tape two or three of the next size flower in a similar fashion to the stem of the spray, followed by three or five large flowers with corollas (*diagram 4J*).

☐ End with as many of the old flowers as you wish.

☐ Paint the stem blueish-violet to blend with the colour of the flowers.

Diagram 4
Making the purple wreath.

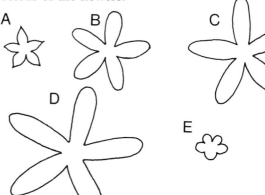

Diagram 5
Templates for the purple wreath.

Chrysanthemum

Intermediate chrysanthemum cultivars are semi-reflexed or partially incurved, i.e. their petals curve back to form a globular-shaped bloom (*plate 3*). The outside petals, however, usually droop.

Small flowers

☐ Cover a piece of 26-gauge wire with green florist's tape and bend a small hook at one end (*diagram 6A*). Mould a small piece of white flower paste into a ball 5 mm in diameter over the hook and set aside to dry completely (*diagram 6B*).

☐ Roll some paste out thinly, cut it out (*diagram 6C and 8A*) and place on a piece of sponge. Roll a small ball tool from the tip to the base of each petal to make it curve inwards (*diagram 6D*).

☐ Brush the dried ball of flower paste with egg white and push the wire end through the centre of the group of petals. Fold them over the ball to form the first round of petals (*diagram 6E*).

☐ Repeat the second step, using a larger template (*diagram 8B*). Secure it to the first round of petals with egg white (*diagram 6F*).

☐ Repeat the previous step, but attach the round of petals upside down to form the drooping petals (*diagram 6G*).

Diagram 6
Making the small
chrysanthemum.

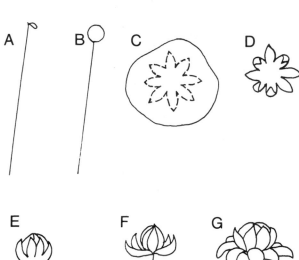

☐ Roll out some green flower paste and cut out a calyx (*diagrams 6H* and *8C*). Secure it to the back of the flower with egg white (*diagram 6I*).

Large flowers
☐ Cover a piece of 22-gauge wire with green florist's tape and bend a small hook at one end (*diagram 7A*). Mould a 15-mm ball of flower paste in the colour you require over the hook, forming a dome shape (*diagram 7B*).
☐ Using a small pair of scissors and holding it at an angle, cut a row of petals from the ball as illustrated (*diagram 7C*). Open the petals out and flatten them between the tips of your thumb and index finger.
☐ Hold the scissors upright and cut a second row of petals into the paste, above the first row (*diagram 7D*). Do not thin these petals, but press them into shape.
☐ Fold the outside petals over the inside ones and set the bud aside to dry completely (*diagram 7E*).

☐ Roll a piece of paste out thinly, cut it out (*diagram 7F* and *9A*) and place it on a piece of sponge. Roll a small ball tool from the tip to the base of each petal to make it curve inwards (*diagram 7G*).
☐ Brush the dried bud with egg white and push the wire end through the centre of the group of petals (*diagram 7H*). Fold them loosely over the bud and hang the bloom upside down to dry slightly.
☐ Repeat the last two steps and attach this round of petals to the flower (*diagram 7I*).
☐ Repeat the previous step twice for each next size template (*diagrams 9B-9D*), but do not hang the flower upside down after the last two rounds have been attached. Rest it upright on a ring of foam rubber, and place small balls of cotton wool between the petals to open them out slightly and keep them separate (*diagram 7J*). Set aside to dry completely.
☐ Roll out a piece of green flower paste and cut out two calyxes (*diagram 9E*). Thin the sepals, leaving the bases thickened. Secure them to the back of the flower with egg white, placing the sepals of the outer calyx between the spaces of the inner ones (*diagram 7K*).

Leaves
☐ Roll a ball of green flower paste into a sausage (*diagram 10A*) and flatten it on both sides with a roller, leaving a short ridge at the base.
☐ Cut out a leaf with a template (*diagram 10B*) and insert a piece of 28-gauge wire into the ridge, about 10 mm deep. Place the leaf upside down on a veiner and press it with a piece of foam rubber to make an impression of veins.
☐ Remove the leaf from the veiner and place on crumpled-up plastic to allow it to take on the shape of a naturally curving leaf (*diagram 10C*).
☐ Make as many as required.

Hint
A piece of foam rubber, with indentations like those in bath mats, is excellent for drying leaves.

A

B

C

D

E

F

G

H

Diagram 7
Making the large chrysanthemum.

I

J

K

A   B   C

Diagram 8
Templates for the small chrysanthemum.

15

Diagram 9
Templates for the
large chrysanthemum.

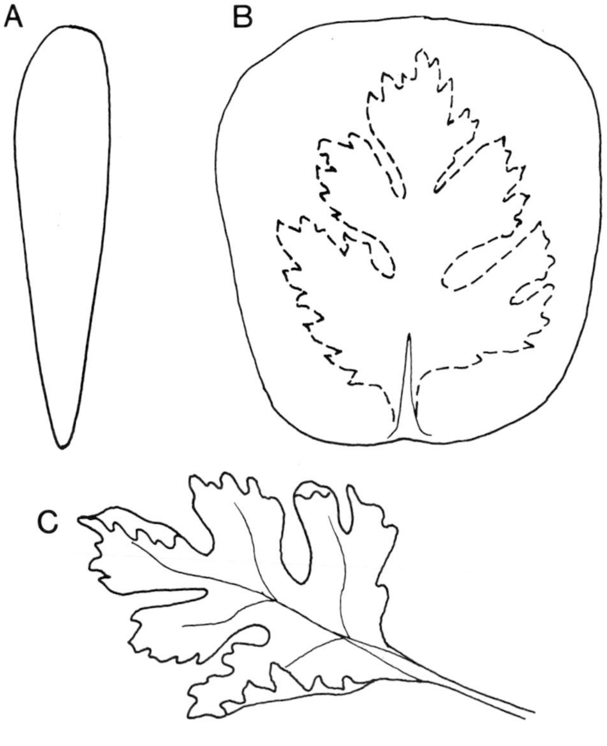

A

C

B

D

E

Diagram 10
Making the leaves of
the chrysanthemum.

A

B

C

Cattleya orchid

The plant bears large individual flowers (*plate 4*), and the hybrids are available in an amazing variety of colours.

Column
☐ Bend a small hook at one end of a piece of 28-gauge wire and mould a 12-mm ball of flower paste into a teardrop shape (of about 20 mm in length) over the hook.
☐ Flatten the underside lengthways, widening but not lengthening it. Shape the top end into a point and make two incisions on either side. Pinch the back of the half teardrop to form a ridge from tip to base (*diagram 11A*). Set aside to dry thoroughly.

Labellum (trumpet)
☐ Roll out a piece of paste thinly (but not transparently thin) and cut out the labellum with a template (*diagrams 11B and 12A*). Place the labellum over an orchid veiner and press it with a piece of foam rubber to obtain an impression.
☐ Make the edge as frilly as possible right round by rolling an anger tool backwards and forwards in one place (*diagram 11C*).
☐ Fold the labellum around the column, securing it with egg white (*diagram 11D*). Allow to set in a cone made of aluminium foil (*diagram 11E*). (*Note:* The column in a fresh flower is hardly visible, and the ridged back is very close to the labellum.)

Petals
☐ Roll a piece of flower paste into a sausage (*diagram 11F*) and flatten on either side with a roller, leaving a short ridge at the base.
☐ Cut out a petal (*diagrams 11G and 12B*), place it upside down on an orchid veiner and press it with a piece of foam rubber to get an impression. Ruffle the edge with an anger tool and pinch the upper side to form a ridge from tip to base (*diagram 11H*).
☐ Insert a piece of 28-gauge wire in the ridge at the base of each petal and allow to dry over a slightly curved object.
☐ Make a second petal the same way, but a mirror image.

Dorsal and lateral sepals
☐ Roll a piece of flower paste into a sausage (*diagram 11I*) and flatten on either side with a roller, leaving a short ridge at the base. Cut out a sepal, the thin point lying on the ridge (*diagrams 11J and 12C*).
☐ Using a veining tool, draw a line from tip to

base down the centre of the sepal. Pinch the back all along this line, deepening the vein. Thin the edges with a ball tool and draw several more indistinct veins on the upper side of the sepal (*diagram 11K*). Insert a piece of 28-gauge wire in the ridge.

☐ Make two more sepals.

☐ Allow to dry with the dorsal sepal curving slightly forwards and the two lateral sepals curving slightly backwards.

Assembling and finishing the orchid

☐ The labellum is often brightly coloured, in complete contrast to the rest of the flower, bright yellow within plain white, for instance. (Artistic licence may be used to dust and/or paint it according to the requirements of the cake.)

☐ First tape the two petals and labellum, and then the three sepals, together. The lateral sepals hang down to the left and right underneath the labellum, and the dorsal sepal comes at the top between the two petals (*diagram 11L*).

☐ Curve the stem and cover it with green flower paste before setting the flower aside to dry completely.

Double gypsophila

This delightful genus contains myriads of small white, frothy flowers (*plate 4*). Cake decorators often use poetic licence and colour them to tone in with the overall colour scheme of the cake.

☐ Roll out a piece of flower paste and cut out a round of petals (*diagram 13A*). Place it on a piece of sponge and roll out the petals with a small ball tool to cup and curl them.

☐ Repeat previous step, but use a smaller template (*diagram 13B*) and cup the petals so that the round takes on a globular shape. Attach it to the first round with egg white.

☐ If the flower is to be used on its own, pull a stamen through it, attaching the anther with egg white. (Make as many as required.) Alternatively, make a number of heads, set them aside to dry and attach them to real thinned-out twigs of dried gypsophila.

Plate 4
A cattleya orchid posy with double gypsophilas, maidenhair fronds and small five-petalled blossoms.

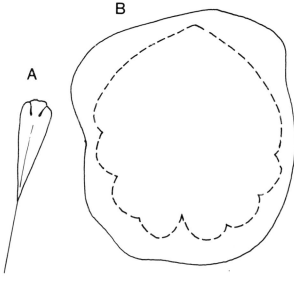

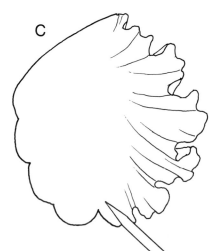

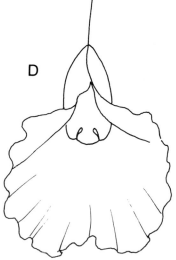

Diagram 11
Making the cattleya orchid.

17

Diagram 11 (continued)

E

I   J   K

F   G

L

H

A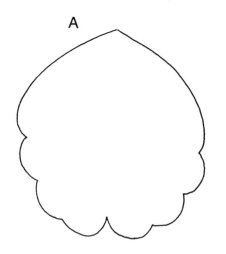

B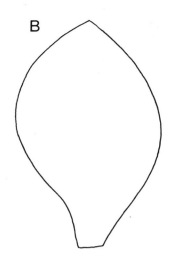

C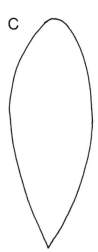

Diagram 12
Templates for the catt-
leya orchid.

Diagram 13
Templates for the
double gypsophila.

A B

Bank's rose *(Rosa banksiae)*

This rose is a vigorous climber and bears double white or yellow flowers *(plate 5)*.

Flower

☐ Bend a small hook at one end of a piece of 28-gauge wire *(diagram 14A)*. Mould a piece of yellow flower paste into the shape of a cone, about 5 mm long and 3 mm wide at the base, over the hook *(diagram 14B)*. Allow to dry.

☐ Roll out some yellow flower paste thinly and cut it out with a template *(diagram 14C)*. Work the edges of each petal with a ball tool and cup them slightly *(diagram 14D)*. Pull the wire supporting the cone through the centre, attaching it with egg white.

☐ Fold alternate petals around the cone *(diagram 14E)*, then fold the remaining three petals over the first three petals to form a bud *(diagram 14F)*. *(Note:* If necessary, make incisions between the petals to facilitate folding.)

☐ Using flower paste coloured a slightly paler shade of yellow, cut out a second shape. Cup the petals as described previously and repeat previous step.

☐ Cut out a third shape in an even paler shade of yellow, cup its petals a little more than before, apply some egg white in the centre and attach it to the flower, but do not close the petals over the second row.

☐ Hang the rose upside down until the outside petals have become firm *(diagram 14G)*, moving them apart with a paintbrush whenever they close up, then set the flower aside, upright, to dry completely.

☐ Attach a 2-mm ball of green flower paste to the back of the rose, using egg white.

☐ Cut out a calyx *(diagrams 14H* and *14I)*, thin out the sepals with a ball tool and cup them

slightly, then make a hollow in the centre with the ball tool.

☐ Pull the flower stalk through the calyx and attach the sepals to the petals with egg white. Make sure that the green ball of paste is completely covered, to form the rose hip *(diagram 14J)*.

☐ These little rambler roses can be used singly or in clusters, depending on the requirements of your arrangement.

Leaves

☐ Roll a piece of green flower paste into a sausage *(diagram 15A)* and flatten it on either side with a roller, leaving a short ridge at the base.

☐ Cut out a long leaf *(diagram 15B)* and insert a piece of fuse wire covered with green florist's tape about 2 mm deep into the ridge. Place the leaf upside down on a veiner or the back of a real

Plate 5
An arrangement of bauhinias and Bank's roses.

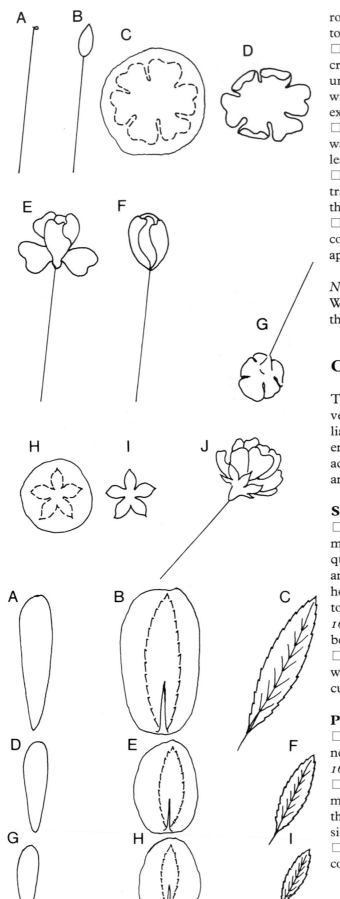

Diagram 14
Making the Bank's
rose.

Diagram 15
Making the leaves of
the Bank's rose.

rose leaf and press it with a piece of foam rubber to get an impression of veins (*diagram 15C*).
☐ Remove it from the veiner and place it on crumpled-up plastic to dry in the shape of a naturally curved leaf. (*Hint:* A piece of foam rubber, with indentations like those in bath mats, is excellent for drying leaves.)
☐ Make two pairs of smaller leaves in the same way (*diagrams 15D-15I*), to obtain a set of five leaves in three different sizes. Set aside to dry.
☐ Tape the larger pair of leaves to the big central leaf, about 2 mm from its base, followed by the smaller pair, about 6 mm further down.
☐ Dust the leaves with brown or red powdered colouring to give them a more natural appearance.

Note
When taping the fuse wire, use only an eighth of the width of green florist's tape.

Camel's foot *(Bauhinia variegata)*

This plant is also known as the orchid tree. Its veined flowers bloom in spring just before the foliage appears. The petals vary in colour from lavender to reddish-purple and measure up to 10 cm across (*plate 5*). The cultivar 'Candida' is smaller and has white flowers.

Stamens (five)
☐ Use two pieces of fuse or 32-gauge wire, each measuring about 62 mm, and tape them with a quarter of the width of florist's tape. Form anthers by bending the top 12 mm of each wire horizontally and folding them back on themselves to obtain crossbars 8 mm in length (*diagrams 16A-16C*). Dip the crossbars in a pale shade of beige royal icing (*diagram 16D*). Set aside to dry.
☐ Repeat previous step, using three pieces of wire each measuring about 72 mm. When dry, curve the stamens as illustrated (*diagram 16E*).

Pistil
☐ Use a 65-mm length of wire, the same thickness as before, and bend it as illustrated (*diagram 16F*).
☐ Mould a 6-mm ball of flower paste around the middle of the wire, about 8 mm below the tip of the curve, forming a pod-shaped ovary with flat sides.
☐ Set aside to dry, then dust with lime-green colouring powder.

20

Petals

☐ Roll a piece of white flower paste, about 20 mm in diameter, into a sausage (*diagram 16G*) and flatten it on either side with a roller, leaving a short ridge at the base. Cut out a petal (*diagrams 16H* and *17A*), then thin out and ruffle the edges slightly with a ball tool. Draw a distinct principal vein down the centre, followed by subsidiary veins fanning out towards the edges. Insert a piece of 32-gauge wire about 10 mm deep into the ridge. Cut base end into a sharp point to ensure that when it is assembled with the other petals, they will fit snugly around the stamens (*diagram 16I*). Make four petals altogether, one pair a mirror image of the other.

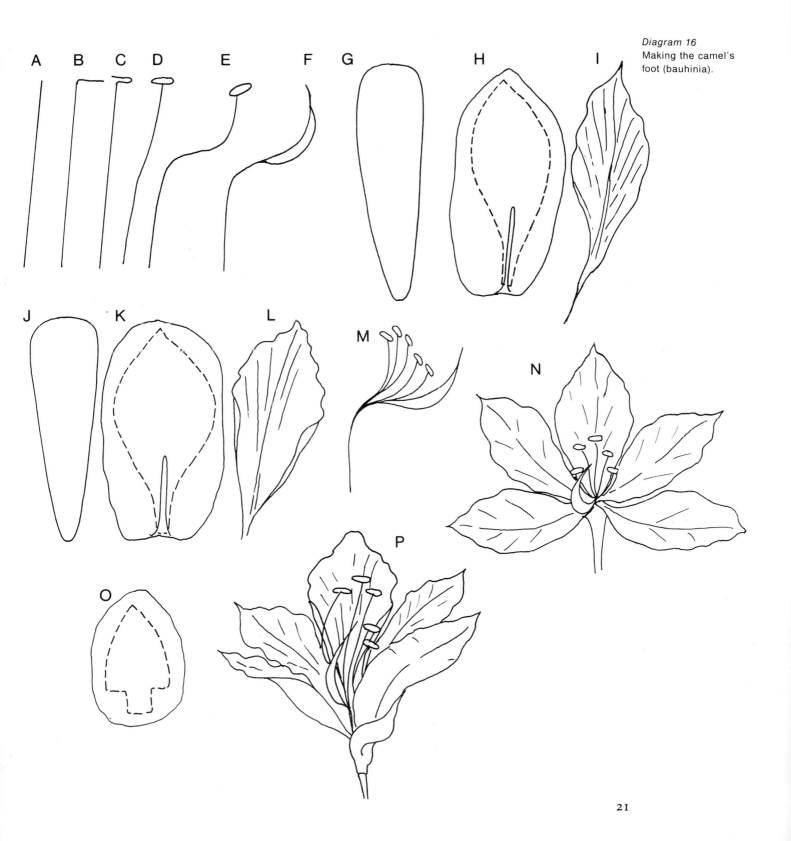

Diagram 16
Making the camel's foot (bauhinia).

Diagram 17
Templates for the ca-
mel's foot (bauhinia).

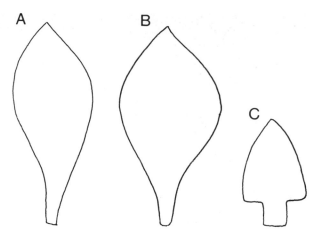

A B C

□ Repeat previous step, but use *diagram 17B* for template (see also *diagrams 16J-16L*). Fold the lower edges of the petal inwards to form a shallow trumpetlike shape. Place in a cone-shaped petal former, or a cone made from aluminium foil, and set aside to dry. (Make one only.)

Assembling the flower
□ Tape the pistil and five stamens together as illustrated (*diagram 16M*).
□ Tape the centre petal to these, the stigma pointing towards its tip, followed by the remaining two pairs of petals, their bulges towards the pistil (*diagram 16N*).

Calyx
□ Roll out green flower paste (not too thinly) and cut out the calyx (*diagrams 16O* and *17C*). Work with a ball tool until it forms a cupped shape. Place over your index finger and draw parallel lines with a veining tool from the tip to the base.
□ Attach it to the base of the petals with the apex slightly to the right of the centre petal. Work the paste down and around the stem to cover about 15 mm (*diagram 16P*).
□ Dust the lower 20 mm of the centre petal with lime green colouring powder.

Blushing bride *(Serruria florida)*

The blushing bride bears nodding, drooping heads of white petal-like bracts, blushed with soft pink (*plate 6*). It has divided leaves, crowded towards the tips of the branches as if clasping the blooms.

Centre
□ Roll a piece of paste into a sausage about 15 mm in length and 5 mm in diameter. Secure it with egg white to one end of a piece of 24-gauge wire covered with green florist's tape, and set aside to dry (*diagram 18A*).
□ Using a No. o tube and white royal icing, pipe lengthways lines right around the sausage, making it about 10 mm in diameter. Pipe small dots on top of the sausage to resemble the tips of the stamens (*diagram 18B*).
□ Tease a piece of cotton wool, cut it into fine fluff and attach it to the top of the sausage with egg white. Set aside to dry.
□ Roll out a piece of white flower paste very thinly and cut it into a rectangle measuring about 18 mm × 50 mm. Cut narrow wedges from the strip, leaving a width of about 3 mm intact, to obtain a comblike shape (*diagram 18C*).
□ Paint the base of the sausage with egg white and wrap the jagged strip twice around it, ensuring that the points of the second row fall in the spaces of the first row. (*Note:* The tips of the wedges must just reach the top of the sausage.) Alternatively, cut out a number of wedges and attach them individually, in two rows. (See *diagram 18D*.) Hang upside down to dry.
□ When dry, draw a fine pink line lengthways down each wedge.
□ Paint the sides of the wedges with egg white and roll them in teased and cut cotton wool. Set aside to dry and, if necessary, cut away the excess fluff.
□ Dust the top of the completed centre with pale pink colouring powder.
□ To make the stamens, roll a length of very pale pink and very pale cream cotton thread twenty times around your index and middle fingers, or use very pale cream thread only and wind it forty times around the two fingers (*diagram 18E*). Remove and fold into a figure 8.
□ Secure the centre with fuse wire (*diagram 18F*), then cut the loops and attach to the base of the centre with egg white. Arrange the stamens evenly around the base and tape the fuse wire to the stem with green florist's tape (*diagram 18G*). (*Note:* Use an eighth of the width of the tape to avoid making the stem too thick.) Cut the stamens about 2 mm shorter than the centre, and paint their tips with reddish-brown vegetable colouring to resemble anthers.

Perianth segments
□ Roll out a piece of white flower paste very thinly and cut out a set of petals (*diagram 18H*). Place it on a piece of foam rubber and cup each petal with a ball tool, then draw principal veins

down their centres. Cut a hole in the centre of the round for the stem of the flower, using a No. 3 writing tube (*diagram 18I*). (*Note:* If the hole is not big enough, you'll break the petals when you insert the wire.) Turn the tips of the petals slightly outwards, and dust the centre of the round as well as the front and the back of the petals at the base with pale lime-green colouring powder. Dust the tips of the petals very pale pink. Paint a faint pink line down the centre, front and back, of each petal. Place the round of petals in a paper cup, about 40 mm in diameter at the top and 25 mm at the bottom (*diagram 18J*), and allow to dry thoroughly.

☐ Repeat previous step to obtain two similar sets of petals.

☐ Repeat step again, but use a smaller cutter (*diagram 18K*). Make only one set of petals this size.

☐ Roll a piece of white flower paste into a sausage. Roll it first to one and then to the other side, leaving a short ridge at the base. Cut out a petal (*diagram 18L*) and insert a short piece of fuse wire into the ridge. Secure firmly. Cup and vein the petal, and set it aside to dry. Make two more petals. Dust base of each petal, front and back, with lime-green and the tips with pale pink colouring powder, then paint a faint pink line down their centres, front and back.

Assembling the flower

☐ Paint the base of the stamens with egg white, pull the stem through the centre of one of the larger sets of petals, attaching the two parts (*diagram 18M*).

☐ To separate the first round of petals from the second, wind green florist's tape round and round the stem until about 3 mm in diameter, then press the ball of tape firmly against the flower. Paint the base of the ball with egg white and attach the next matching set, arranging its petals so that they fall between the spaces of those on the first round.

☐ Attach the third and smaller set of petals in the same way, separating them with a ball of green florist's tape.

☐ Tape the three individual petals 1 mm apart in a spiral around the stem at the base of the flower (*diagram 18N*). (*Note:* For a specimen flower, more of the individual petals can be added, making them gradually smaller and colouring them pale green, leaving out the blush of pink.)

Plate 6
Blushing brides.

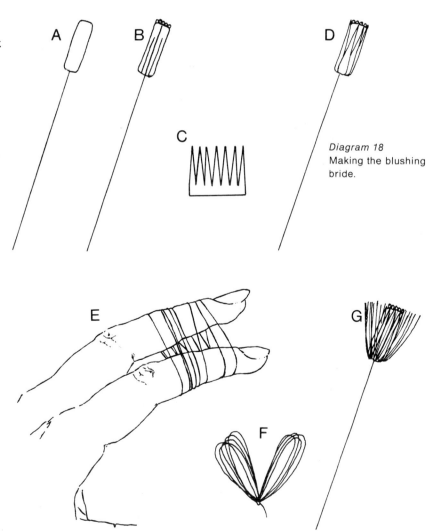

Diagram 18
Making the blushing bride.

23

Diagram 18 (continued)

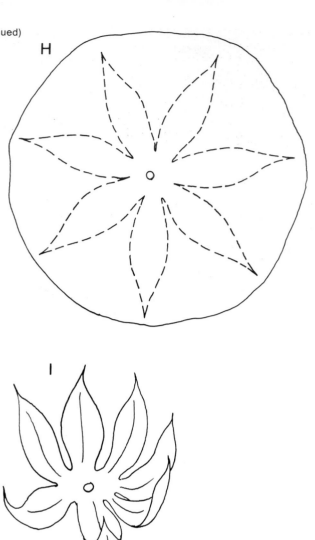

Leaves

To make the delicate feathery leaves of the blushing bride, twist thin strips of florist's tape into spirals and then twist these together as illustrated (*diagram 18N*).

Wallflower *(Cheiranthus cheiri)*

Wallflowers come in a number of varieties and a wide selection of colours – white, golden brown and different shades of yellow, purple, pink and red (*plate 7*). The blooms measure about 20 mm across and are grouped together on a stem.

Bloom

☐ Bend a small hook at one end of a piece of 32-gauge wire and mould a 5-mm ball of maroon flower paste into a sausage 10 mm × 2 mm around it (*diagrams 19A-19C*). Form the ovary by making an indentation about 2 mm above the base, using a pin held horizontally.

☐ Hollow out the top part of the sausage by inserting a toothpick or similar instrument into the paste. Make four evenly spaced slits, each about

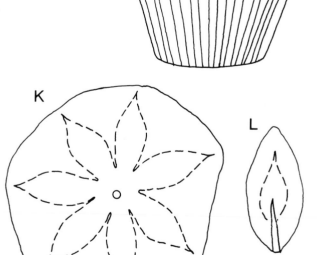

3 mm long, around the upper edge. Cut each section to a point, thus forming the calyx of the flower (*diagrams 19D and 19E*). Set aside to dry.

☐ Roll out yellow flower paste thinly and cut out four petals (*diagrams 19F and 20*). Thin the edges with a ball tool and draw a principal vein down the centre, followed by a network of radiating smaller veins (*diagram 19G*).

☐ Cup the petals slightly and attach to the calyx with egg white. Set aside to dry.

☐ Place five stamens, each about 2 mm in length, in the heart of the flower, then dust the petals with dark yellow, brown or purple colouring powder, depending on the variety you are making.

☐ Use the flowers singly or in groupings (*diagram 19H*).

Bud
Mould a 5-mm ball of maroon flower paste into the shape of an upside-down teardrop over the anther of a stamen. Set aside to dry.

Note
There are no instructions for leaves as they are seldom used.

China flower (*Adenandra villosa*)

This plant develops showy terminal flowers with roundish, shiny white petals suffused with red (*plate 8*). Red glands are borne at the ends of the stamens, and the leaves and sepals are flat (*diagram 19H*).

Calyx
☐ Mould a piece of flower paste into the shape of a hat with a wide brim and a pointed crown, 10 mm high × 3 mm across at the base, and cut out the calyx (*diagrams 21A and 22A*).

☐ Thin the sepals with a ball tool and hollow out the tube with a toothpick.

☐ Pull a piece of 28-gauge wire through the calyx and attach it with egg white (*diagrams 21B and 21C*). Set aside to dry.

Petals
☐ Roll out white flower paste thinly and cut out five petals (*diagrams 21D and 22B*).

☐ Stretch and thin out each petal by working it with a ball tool in the palm of your hand, then draw a principal vein down the centre from tip to base.

☐ Attach the petals to the calyx with egg white, placing them slightly overlapping between the sepals (*diagram 21E*). Set aside to dry.

☐ Use reddish-pink colouring powder and draw a line down the centre of each petal, starting with a point at the tip and becoming wider towards the base.

☐ Turn the flower over and dust the back of the petals and calyx with the same shade of colouring powder.

☐ Pipe a little green royal icing in the throat of the calyx and insert eight short, red stamens in it,

Plate 7
Close-up of wall flowers on a fantasy wedding cake with mice.

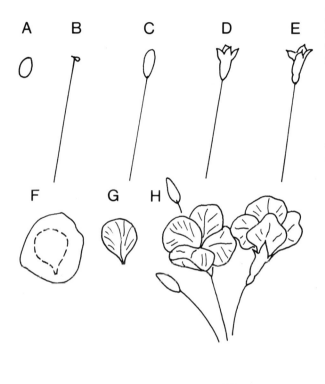

Diagram 19
Making the wallflower.

Diagram 20
Template for the wall-flower.

25

Plate 8
China flowers comple-
menting mice figures
moulded from flower
paste.

Diagram 21
Making the china
flower.

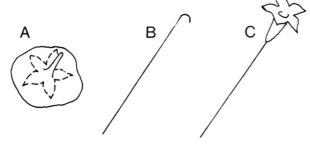

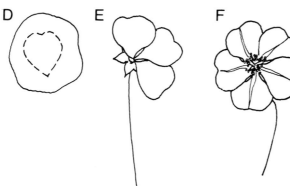

Diagram 22
Templates for the
china flower.

Plate 9
A wild iris in combi-
nation with china
flowers behind a pair
of moulded mice
figures.

letting them protrude about 4 mm. When dry,
brush the tips of the stamens with egg white and
dip them in a mixture of yellow colouring powder and maize-meal to form the pollen (*diagram
21F*).

☐ Use these flowers as fillers in arrangements.

26

Wild iris *(Dietes grandiflora)*

The wild iris (*plate 9*) grows in large clumps and
has six white perianth segments with yellow or
brown markings near the base. The three central
segments are mauve and contain stigmas beneath
which are three stamens. The leaves are dark
green, rigid and sword-shaped, and can be up to
1 m long.

Small perianth segments (make three)

☐ Roll a small piece of mauve flower paste into a
sausage. Flatten it with a roller, first to one and
then to the other side, leaving a small ridge at the
base. Cut out a perianth segment (*diagram 23A*).

☐ Thin the edges with a ball tool, place segment
upside down on a piece of sponge and draw a
central vein from tip to base. Pinch the vein on
the upper side to raise it, then draw radiating
subsidiary veins with an anger tool or toothpick.
Ruffle the edges slightly.

☐ Cover a piece of fuse or 32-gauge wire with
white florist's tape and insert it in the ridge.
Curve the segment as illustrated (*diagram 23B*),
bending the tip slightly towards you. Set aside to
dry. Make two more segments.

☐ Tape the three segments together as in *diagram 23C*. Using white flower paste, make a
thickening about 8 mm in length around the
wires at the base of the segments.

Large perianth segments (make three, plus
three)

☐ Follow first step for small perianth segments,
but use a different template (*diagram 23D*) and

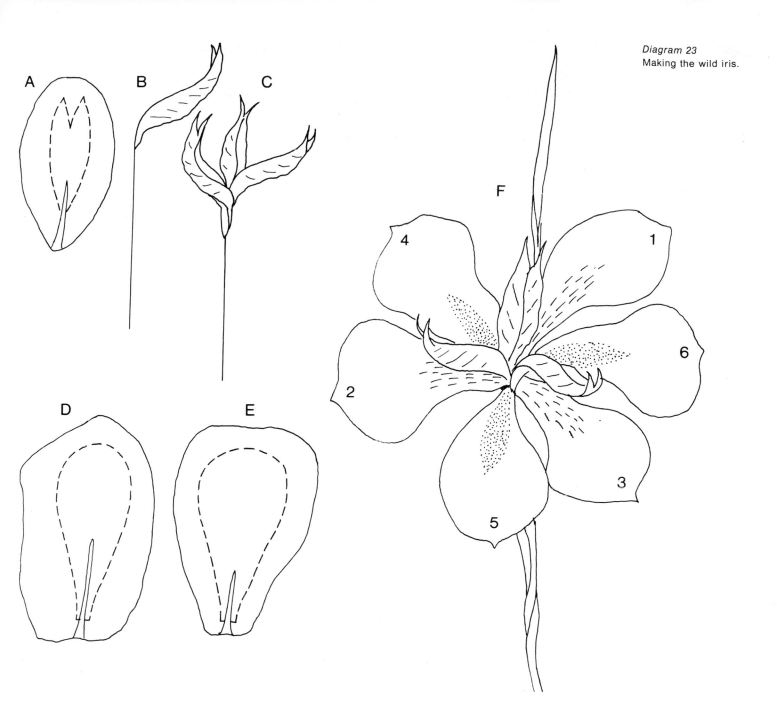

Diagram 23
Making the wild iris.

white flower paste. Thin the edges with a ball tool and draw lengthways veins on the top side (*plate 9*). Ruffle the edges slightly. Cover a piece of fuse or 32-gauge wire with green florist's tape and insert it in the ridge. Curve the lower 15 mm of the segment backwards and set aside to dry. Make two more segments.

☐ Repeat previous step, using a larger template (*diagram 23E*).

☐ When all the segments are dry, paint short dark-brown broken lines over the lower part of the smaller white segments (*Nos. 1-3 in diagram 23F*). Paint the lower part of the larger white segments with yellow colouring and, while still wet, sprinkle some yellow pollen (page 9) over it to create a raised effect (*Nos. 4-6 in diagram 23F*).

Assembling the flower

Tape the three smaller white segments, evenly spaced, around the stem just below the thickening of the mauve segments, followed by the larger white segments, filling the spaces left (*diagram 23F*).

27

right, in a hollow container to form a slightly cupped flower.

Second calyx
☐ Roll out some flower paste thinly (a deeper shade of green than for the first calyx) and cut out a round of sepals (*diagrams 24H* and *25C*).
☐ Roll the tips of the sepals into thin, sharp points, curving and bending them back slightly (*diagram 24I*). Brush the centre with egg white and secure the calyx to the back of the flower (*diagram 24J*). Set aside to dry.

Centre
☐ Using a No. 1 writing tube, pipe tiny blobs of yellow royal icing in the centre of the flower, forming a dome shape.
☐ Insert a circle of short black stamens, about 6 mm in length, around its outside edge (*diagram 24K*).
☐ Using a brush, place a drop of soft yellow royal icing on the tip of each stamen, then dust each with a deeper shade of colouring powder to form pollen.

Leaves
☐ Roll out some green flower paste transparently thin to about 40 mm wide and 70 mm long. Place a piece of taped fuse wire in the centre, securing it with egg white.
☐ Cover with another thin layer of paste and roll out transparently thin to both sides, amalgamating the two layers.
☐ Cut out acute leaves as shown in *diagram 24L* and transfer the stalk with the utmost care to a piece of indented foam rubber so that the leaves can dry in a naturally curving way. (*Note:* Bend the wire slightly while the paste is still pliable to make it look more natural, and if the paste around the wire is too thick, pinch it thinner with a pair of tweezers.)

Assemble the flowers and leaves as required.

Cosmos *(Bidens formosa)*

Cosmos are traditionally white, pink or red (*plate 10*), but new cultivars in bright red and orange are now also available.

First calyx
☐ Bend a small hook at one end of a piece of 26-gauge wire and flatten it to form a horizontal circle (*diagram 24A*).
☐ Mould a piece of flower paste into the shape of a hat with a wide brim and a rounded crown, 7 mm in diameter at the base and 6 mm high.
☐ Cut out a calyx (*diagrams 24B* and *25A*) and thin the sepals with a small ball tool. Make a shallow indentation in the throat.
☐ Dip the bent part of the wire in egg white and push the shaft through the calyx, securing the ring in the paste (*diagram 24C*).

Petals
☐ Use flower paste in the colour of the flower you wish to make and roll it out thinly. Cut out eight petals (*diagrams 24D* and *25B*).
☐ Thin the petals slightly with a ball tool and place them on a flat piece of foam rubber. Draw three distinct lines between the scallops from top end to base of each petal. Draw further short, fine lines down the scalloped edge with light strokes of the veining tool (*diagram 24E*).
☐ Cup the sides of each petal with a ball tool.
☐ Secure the petals to the calyx with egg white (*diagrams 24F* and *24G*) and allow to dry, up-

28

A

B

C

D

E

F

Diagram 24
Making the cosmos.

G

H

I

J

K

L

A

B

C

Diagram 25
Templates for the cosmos.

29

Forget-me-not *(Myosotis)*

The name is said to be derived from a German legend about a knight who, while gathering flowers on the bank of a river for his beloved, fell into the water and was swept away by the current. As he vanished, he cried out: "Forget me not!" Be that as it may, the flower develops from a pinkish colour when young to a deep blue, but there are also white and pink varieties *(plate 36)*.

Bloom
☐ Mould a 5-mm ball of white flower paste into the shape of a hat with a pointed crown and wide brim, and cut out bloom with a template *(diagrams 26A, 26B and 27)*.
☐ Thin the petals with a ball tool and hollow out the trumpet with a toothpick *(diagrams 26C and 26D)*.

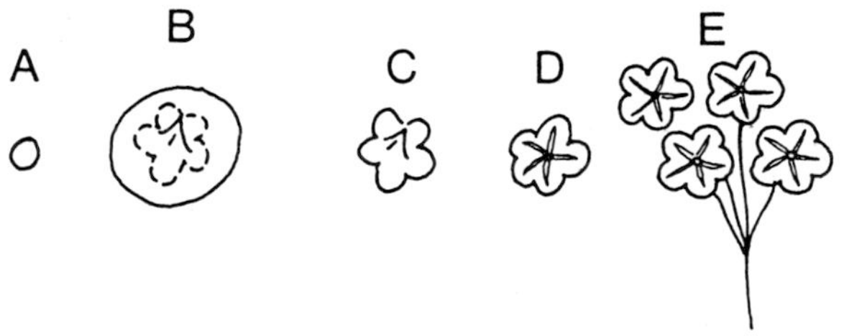

☐ Pull a fine stamen through the flower until the yellow anther rests in the throat, and set aside to dry.
☐ Dust the edges of the petals, front and back, with blue colouring powder, leaving a white star in the centre of the flower.

Calyx
Paint the base of the flower with green vegetable colouring, as it is too small to make from paste.

Bud
☐ Mould a 3-mm ball of white flower paste into the shape of a teardrop over the anther of a fine stamen.
☐ When dry, dust with blue colouring powder and, as for the bloom, paint a calyx at the base.

Note
Be sure to use stamens with bright yellow anthers. Assemble the blooms and buds into clusters, or tape them together into a spray *(diagram 26E)*. There are no instructions for leaves, as they are seldom used.

Diagram 26
Making the forget-me-not.

Diagram 27
Template for the forget-me-not.

Cakes for various occasions

Wedding cakes

Plate 11

Wedding cake with purple wreath and chrysanthemums. Interesting features of this cake are the double lace points along the top border (*diagram 61J*) and the royal icing ribbon insertions which carry through the colour of the flowers. Figure-piped doves add a romantic touch, a theme repeated in the embroidery on the side of the cake (*diagram 48*). The top cake measures 150 mm × 150 mm (6 in. × 6 in.) and was cut from the larger cake, which measures 300 mm × 300 mm (12 in. × 12 in.). (For making the flowers, see pages 12-14.)

Plate 12

Wedding cake with bride and groom. This is a versatile design, as the bottom layer can be used on its own as a single-tier cake for a small wedding (*plate 13*). The figures were made according to the Mexican method, which is not described in this book, but could also be made using moulds (page 8-9). A total of 29 Bank's roses (page 19), 17 rosebuds, 75 anonymous flowers, 12 bauhinias (page 20), 20 sprays of hyacinths, 24 sprays of five-petalled blossoms and 29 miniature azaleas were used for the arrangements. (For the embroidery pattern, see *diagram 50*.)

Plate 13
Bottom tier of wedding cake with bride and groom.

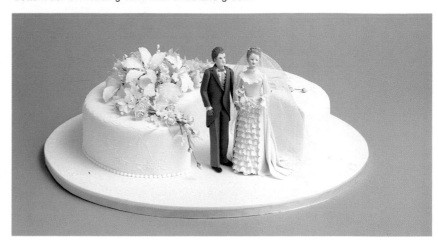

Plate 14
Close-up of wedding cake with bride and groom.

Plate 15
Close-up of embroidery work on wedding cake with bride
and groom.

Plate 16
Kidney-shaped wedding cake in bas-relief. The floral arrangements on this cake consist of cattleya orchids (page 16), double gypsophila (page 17), maidenhair fronds and small five-petalled blossoms. The bride's cotton net veil has a royal-icing edging, while the frill of her dress is continued right around the bottom border. (For the embroidery and lace patterns, see *diagrams 49* and *61I* respectively.)

Plate 17
Two-tiered wedding cake with blushing brides. It consists of an 18 cm² cake combined with a 30 cm² cake cut in two, as can be seen. It is decorated with arrangements of blushing brides (see page 22) and grey leaves. The floral theme is repeated in the embroidery work on the sides of the cakes (*diagram 51*) and is complemented by delicate lace points (*diagram 61A*). The shell borders were made with a No. 42 *Bekenal* tube.

34

Plate 18
Fantasy wedding cake with mice. It is particularly suited to a reception held in a garden. The mushrooms and figures (see page 10-11 for dressing them) were moulded freehand from flower paste. The floral arrangements consist of wallflowers (page 24-25), miniature pansies, lilies of the valley, Bank's roses (page 19-20) and miniature daisies. (For the embroidery pattern, see *diagram 52*.)

Plate 19
Fantasy wedding or anniversary cake with mice. This heart-shaped cake was decorated with extension and bridgework (see *Sugar decorating* by Kate Venter, Tafelberg Publishers, 1987, page 13-14). Agapanthus, china flowers (page 25) and wild irises (page 26) were used for the floral arrangements. The heads of the mice were made using a putty mould (page 9), while their bodies and arms were moulded freehand. (*Note:* The head and arms should be attached as described under *Modelling figures and dressing them*, page 10-11.) When dry, paint the bodies with a brush and very thin coloured royal icing. The cake is finished off with little hearts and musical notes. (For the lace-point pattern, see *diagram 61B*.)

Christening and stork-tea cakes

Plate 20

Baby in bootee. Cut a 23 cm² (9 sq. in.) cake in half and cut a shoe from one piece (*diagram 31A*). Cut the other half in two crossways and place one of the pieces on top of the shoe at the back. Shape the nose and heel, and cover the whole shoe with marzipan. Add a little CMC or gum tragacanth to a mixture of fondant, roll it out to about 5 mm thick and cut out a tongue (*diagram 31B*). Place in position and attach with egg white. Cut the upper of the shoe from the same kind of fondant mixture (*diagram 31C*, using an opened-out pattern piece as per small diagram). Attach upright around the shoe, forming a seam at the heel. Smooth the fondant neatly over the nose. Attach a thin clay-gun cord to the base of the shoe, forming a sole. Make a pillow from flower paste, finish it off with a frill and place it in the shoe. Mould a baby as described on page 10, place it on the pillow and cover it with a blanket made from flower paste. Mould a teddy bear free-hand and place it in position. Attach two ribbons for the laces, and finish off the cake with small floral arrangements (miniature roses, apple blossoms, lilac sprays and anonymous flowers were used in this instance). The edge of the board was crimped and overpiped in a matching colour.

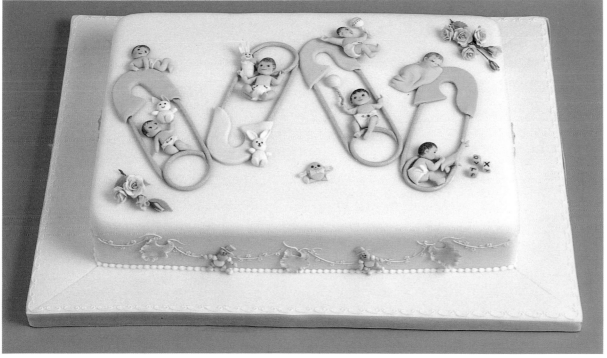

Plate 21 (top)
Cake with baby's bedroom scene. The furniture was made
from pastillage and assembled with royal icing (*diagrams
44A–44K*). The rocking horse (*diagram 44L*) was cut out of
flower paste rolled out to about 5 mm thick. The bear was
moulded free-hand, but could also be made using a plaster
of Paris mould (page 8). An arrangement of roses, carna-
tions, hyacinths and five-petalled blossoms add colour and
balance to the design, while ribbons and bibs made from
flower paste lend an unusual finishing touch to the sides of
the cake.

Plate 22 (below)
Cake with napkin pins. Mould seven babies freehand as described on page 10. Cut the hooks of the safety pins from
flower paste (*diagram 32*) and make the wire parts with a
clay gun. Attach in position and finish off the cake with
miniature roses, bibs and toys.

Novelty and fantasy cakes

Plate 23
A most unusual cake for Mother on any day that is special to her. The pierrot figurine was made according to the Mexican technique, but you could use a porcelain doll instead so Mother could keep it as a gift after the cake has been en- joyed. The card was made from pastillage and combined with an arrangement of white and pink cosmos (page 28). This floral theme is repeated in the lace and embroidery work on the side of the cake (*diagrams 53* and *61H* respectively).

Plate 24
Molly Mouse tending her garden. A plaque in bas-relief. (For
pattern, see *diagram 34*, and for method, page 7.)

Plate 25
Monty Mouse flying his kite. A plaque in bas-relief. (For pattern, see *diagram 35*, and for method, page 7.)

Plate 26
Clive the clown is too big for his boots! A cake for a toddler with a humorous design in bas-relief. (For pattern, see *diagram 36*, and for method, page 7.)

Plate 27
Victoria Plum painting a bee. This plaque serves as an example of how illustrations in children's picture books can be turned into fascinating designs. (For pattern, see *diagram 37*, and for bas-relief method, page 7.) Cynthia Fletcher received a first prize for this on the Cape Show.

Plate 28

Four seasons. The background of the pictures (*plates 29-32*) were done in Australian flood work, and the frames, arches, collar and figures (*diagrams 41-43*) in conventional flood work, a method which is described in *Sugar art* by Kate Venter (Tafelberg Publishers, 1984), p. 28-32. Each panel was made individually and attached in sequence to the sides of the cake. The roping around the base was done with a clay gun. (Cynthia Fletcher devised this cake in 1987 and won three awards for it: best on show at the Cape Show and two gold medals at the *Salon Culinaire*.)

Plate 29
Spring.

Plate 30
Summer.

Plate 31
Autumn.

Plate 32
Winter.

Plate 33
Children playing on
the lawn. The well, the
different components
of the house (*diagrams
47A-47T*) and the um-
brella were cut from
pastillage. (*Note:* The
umbrella was shaped
over a plastic ball.)
Flower paste was used
for the children's
clothes, as well as to
cover a wire network
for the tree. (For mak-
ing and dressing the
figures, see *diagrams
1-3*, page 10-11.)

Plate 34
Close-up of Children playing on the lawn.

Plate 35
Close-up of Children playing on the lawn.

Plate 36
Fantasy cake with fairies. The fairies were made in the same way as the figures in Children playing on the lawn (*diagrams 1-3*, page 10). They represent flowers such as the rose, bluebell, carnation and daisy. Their wings were made by dipping fine wire frames into a solution of 5 ml (1 t) gelatine powder and 10 ml (2 t) water dissolved over heat. (*Note:* When making a frame, leave a little grip by which to handle it. And when lifting it out of the gelatine, take care not to burst the bubble.) Allow it to dry upright by pressing the grip into a piece of polystyrene. The wings may be painted with food colouring when dry. The bridge was cut out of green flower paste, using a loquat leaf as template and veiner.

Plate 37
Close-up of Fantasy cake with fairies.

Cakes for special occasions

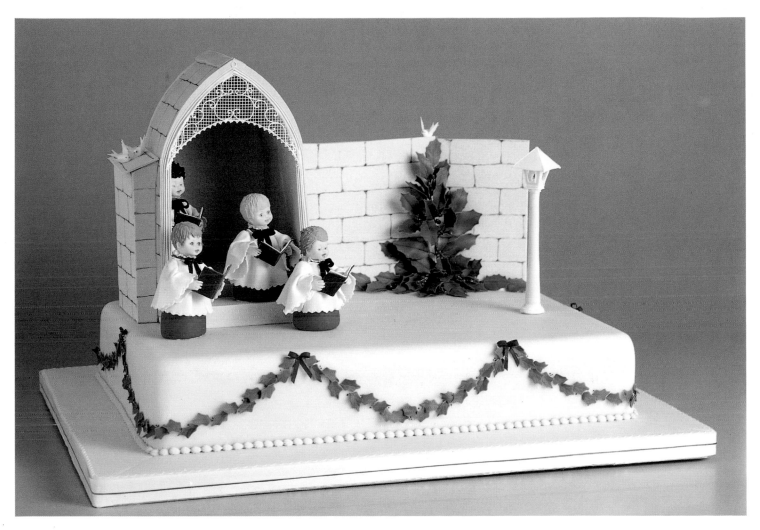

Plate 38
Christmas cake with choir boys. The arch and walls of the church (*diagrams 45A-45N*) as well as the lamppost were made from pastillage. The body of each boy consists of a red flower paste cone over which a surplice was draped (*diagrams 45O-45S*). The hands were moulded freehand, while the heads were made with a plaster of Paris mould (page 8). The covers and pages of the hymn books were made up with layers of green and white modelling paste (*diagram 45T*). A holly tree (leaves on wire taped together) gives balance to the cake, while a couple of doves add a symbolic touch of peace. Garlands of holly leaves and berries caught by little red bows finish the sides of the cake, and a narrow strip of red ribbon the sides of the board.

Plate 39
Madonna in cocoa painting. (See *diagram 29* for pattern.) The roping around the plaque and the base of this Christmas cake was done with a clay gun, while arrangements of Christmas roses (*Helleborus niger*) and holly leaves and berries were added for colour and balance. The floral theme is repeated in the embroidery work on the side of the cake (*diagram 54*).

Plate 40

Occasional cake with roses. The most striking thing about this cake is its elegant simplicity: three roses and three sets of leaves arranged on a plastic icing cloth draped over a round cake and caught with a bow to reveal the adornment of ruffles. The cloth was finished with delicate embroidery work and a picot edging, while the ruffles were made according to the Garrett frill method. (*Note:* A little CMC, gum tragacanth or tylose should be added to the plastic icing mixture to strengthen it.)

Birthday cakes

Plate 41
Cake for a 21st birthday decorated in bas-relief. (*See diagrams 39* and *40* for patterns.) Tiny five-petalled flowers in a variety of colours create a garden effect around the figures, a theme which is repeated on the sides and on the corners of the board. The base of the cake is finished with a shell border (*diagram 55B*), overpiped with a No. 1 writing tube. (For the embroidery pattern, see *diagram 55A* and for the bas-relief method, page 7.)

Plate 42
Close-up of Cake for a 21st birthday decorated in bas-relief. (See *diagram 39* for pattern.)

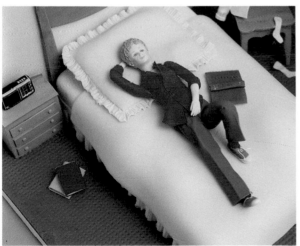

Plate 43
Teenager lounging in his room. The boy was made according to the Mexican method, which is not described in this book, but could also be made with a mould (page 8-9). His clothes were made from flower paste and his duvet cut from a thick layer of plastic icing so as to give a padded effect. The different components of the furniture were cut from pastillage (*diagrams 46A-46R*), while the radio and books were moulded freehand. A 15 cm × 23 cm (6 in. × 9 in.) cake forms the bed.

Plate 44
Close-up of Teenager lounging in his room.

Plate 45
Cake for a girl's 21st birthday decorated with a picture in cocoa painting. White embroidery work (*diagram 56*) on a background of antique white complements the colour of the picture. Arrangements of white daisies add a light, feminine touch, while a snail's trail finishes the bottom border. The key was made with a clay gun and flower paste, and the picture is held up by a pastillage disc. (For embroidery pattern on side of board, see *diagram 57*, and for patterns of picture and key, *diagrams 30A* and *30B*.)

Plate 46
Close-up of embroidery work on Cake for a girl's 21st birthday decorated with a picture in cocoa painting.

54

Plate 47
Occasional cake for a teenage girl. (See *diagram 38* for pattern.) The girl was made in bas-relief (see method on page 7), while her umbrella was cut from flower paste and draped over half a dome shape to dry. The basket was made from royal icing in basket weave and filled with miniature roses. Painted-on stepping stones and clouds finish the cake, and apple blossom arrangements the board.

55

Patterns

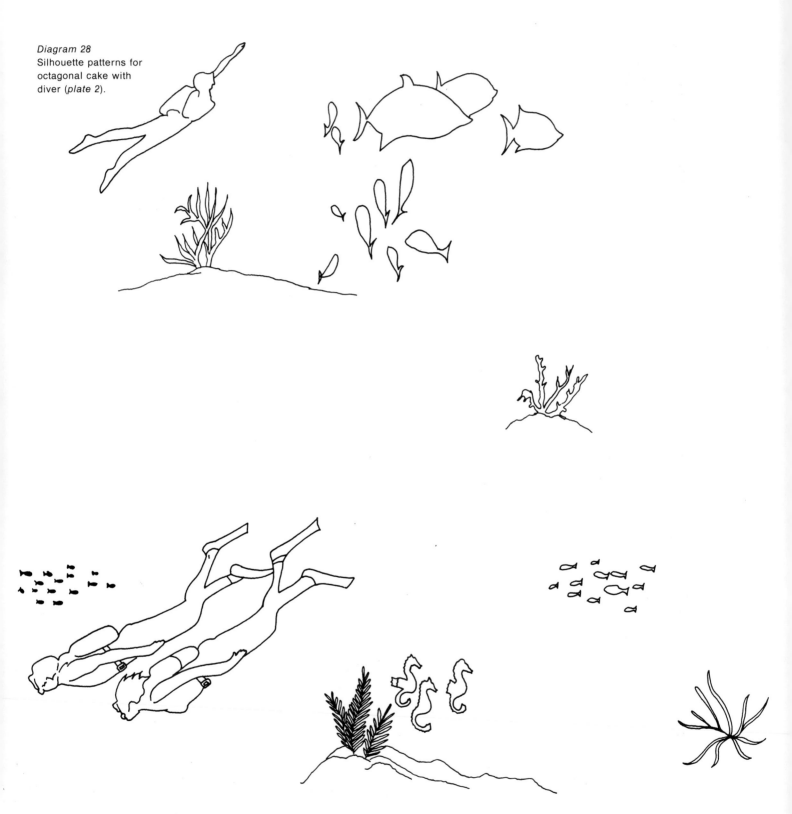

Diagram 28
Silhouette patterns for
octagonal cake with
diver (*plate 2*).

Diagram 29
Pattern for Madonna in
cocoa painting (*plate
39*).

A

Diagram 30
Patterns of picture and
key for girl's 21st birthday cake decorated
with a picture in cocoa
painting (*plate 45*).

B

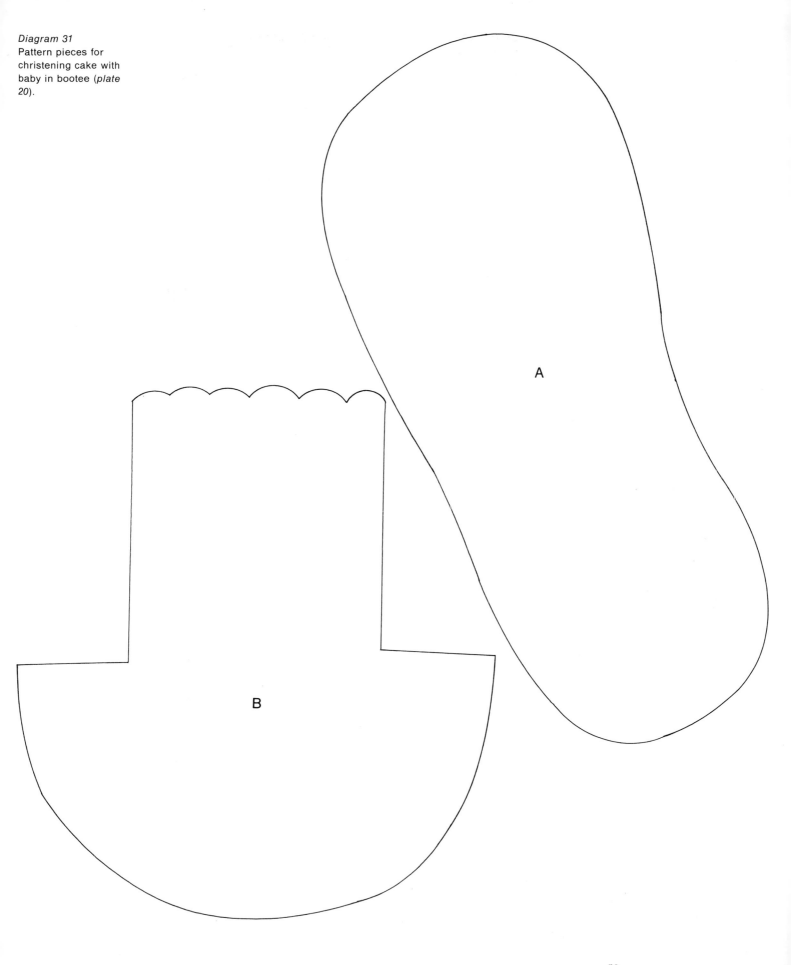

Diagram 31
Pattern pieces for
christening cake with
baby in bootee (*plate
20*).

A

B

Diagram 31 (continued)

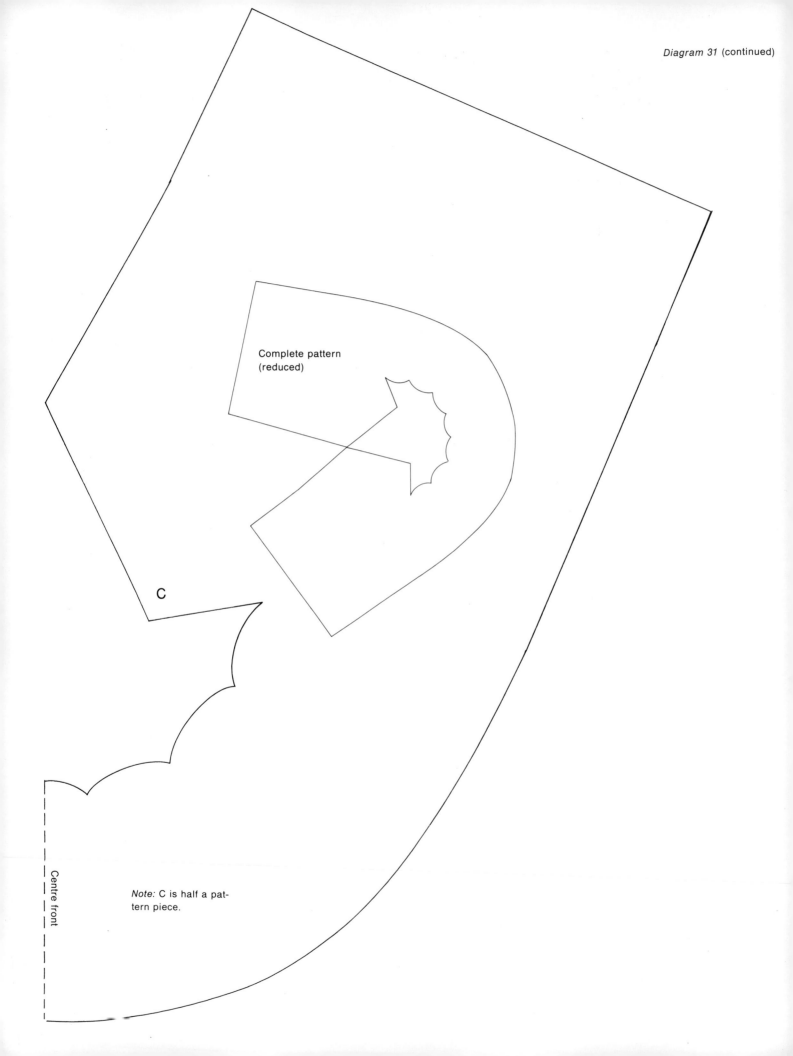

Complete pattern
(reduced)

C

Note: C is half a pat-
tern piece.

Centre front

A

B

Diagram 32
Patterns for christening cake with napkin pins (*plate 22*).

C

D

Diagram 33
Pattern for plaque in
bas-relief (*plate 1*).

Diagram 34
Pattern for Molly
Mouse tending her
garden (*plate 24*).

Diagram 35
Pattern for Monty
Mouse flying his kite
(*plate 25*).

Diagram 36
Pattern for Clive the
clown (*plate 26*).

Diagram 37
Pattern for Victoria
Plum painting a bee
(*plate 27*).

Diagram 38
Pattern for the occasional cake for a teenage girl (*plate 47*).

Diagram 39
Pattern for girl on cake
for a 21st birthday dec-
orated in bas-relief
(*plates 41* and *42*).

Diagram 40
Pattern for boy on
cake for a 21st birth-
day decorated in bas-
relief (*plate 41*).

Diagram 41
Pattern for the arches
on the four seasons
cake (*plate 28*).

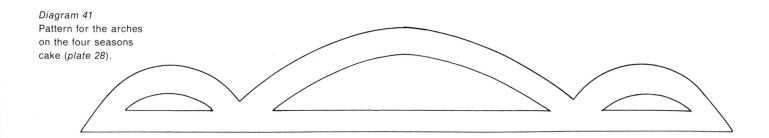

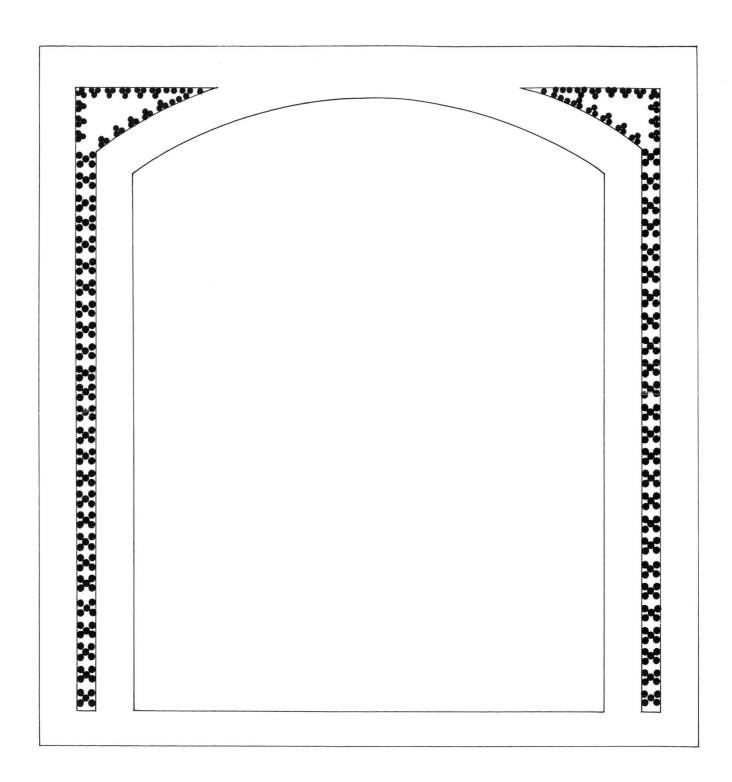

Diagram 42
Pattern for the frames
on the four seasons
cake (*plate 28*).

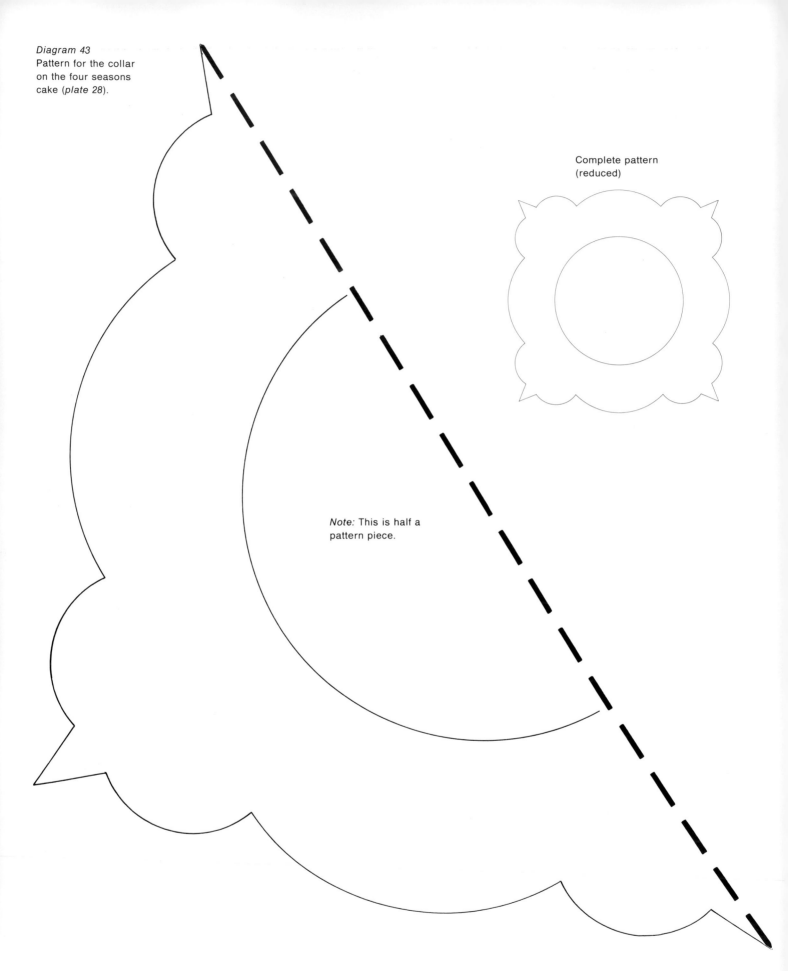

Diagram 43
Pattern for the collar
on the four seasons
cake (*plate 28*).

Complete pattern
(reduced)

Note: This is half a
pattern piece.

70

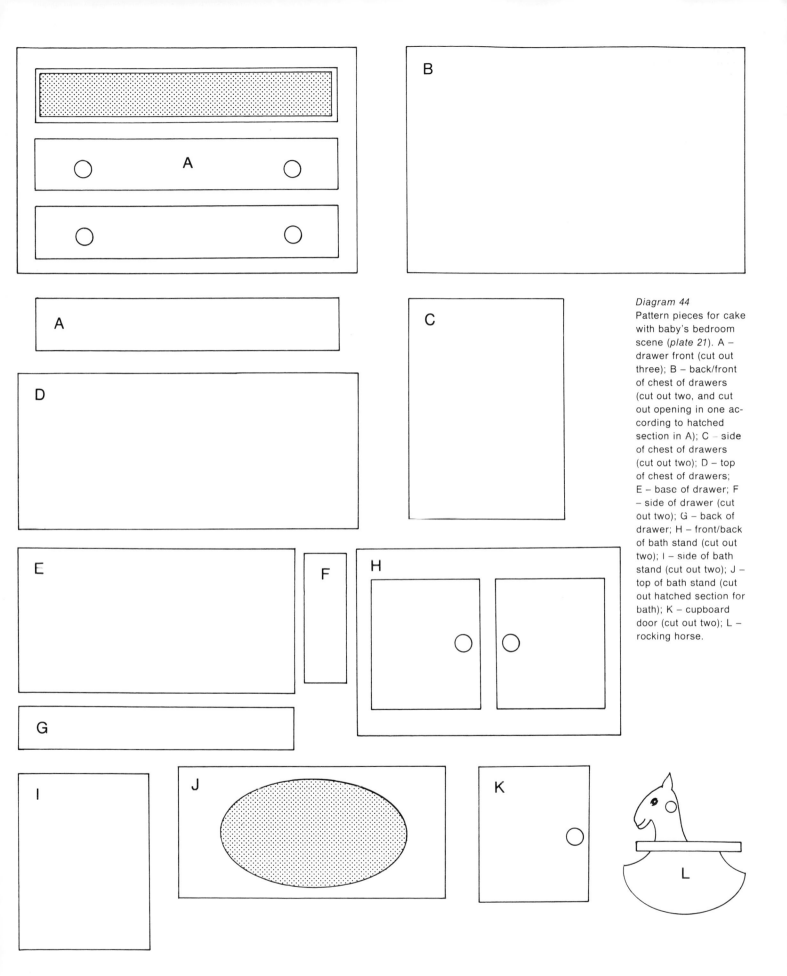

Diagram 44
Pattern pieces for cake with baby's bedroom scene (*plate 21*). A – drawer front (cut out three); B – back/front of chest of drawers (cut out two, and cut out opening in one according to hatched section in A); C – side of chest of drawers (cut out two); D – top of chest of drawers; E – base of drawer; F – side of drawer (cut out two); G – back of drawer; H – front/back of bath stand (cut out two); I – side of bath stand (cut out two); J – top of bath stand (cut out hatched section for bath); K – cupboard door (cut out two); L – rocking horse.

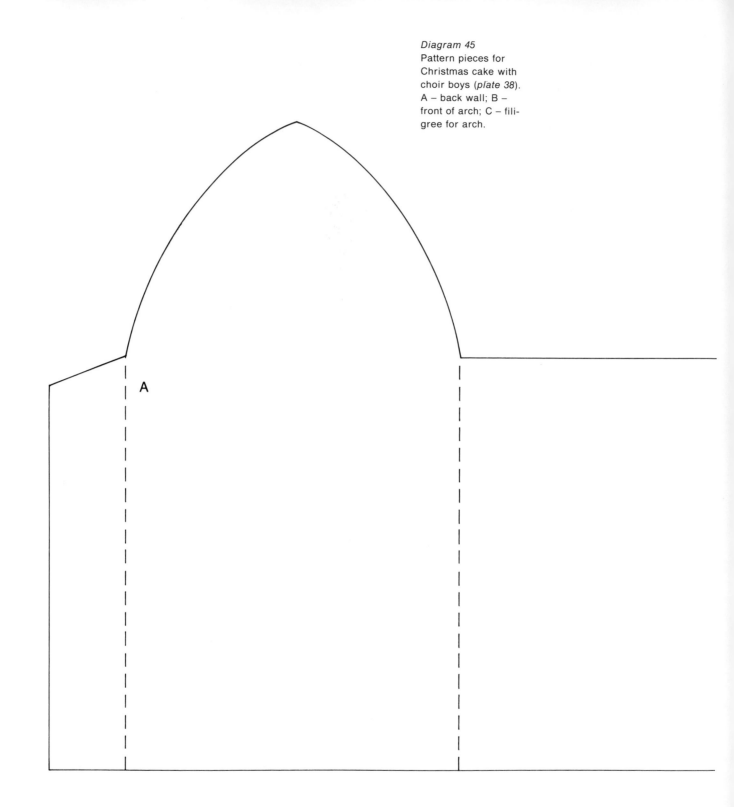

Diagram 45
Pattern pieces for
Christmas cake with
choir boys (*plate 38*).
A – back wall; B –
front of arch; C – fili-
gree for arch.

A

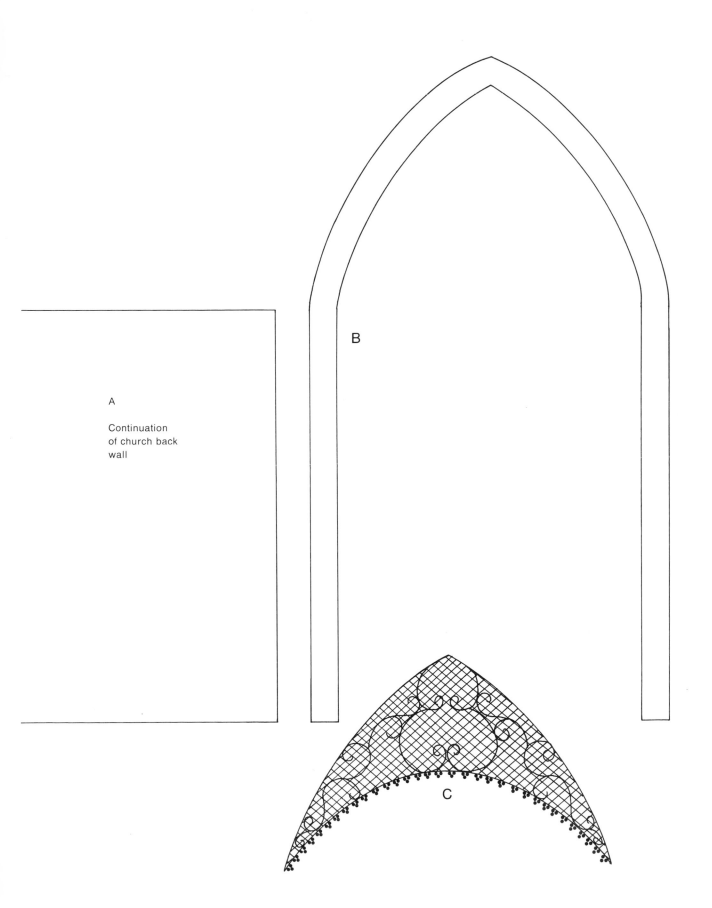

A

Continuation
of church back
wall

B

C

D

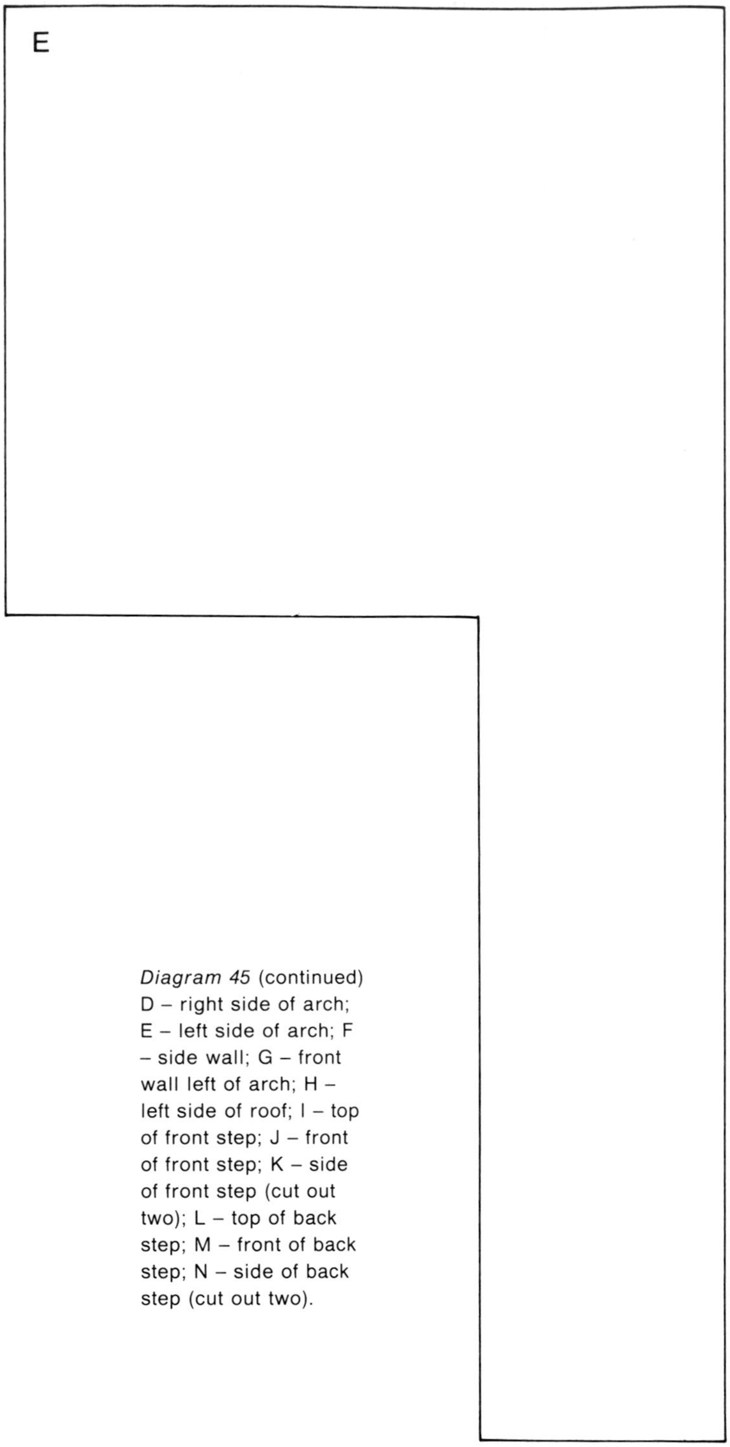

E

Diagram 45 (continued)
D – right side of arch;
E – left side of arch; F
– side wall; G – front
wall left of arch; H –
left side of roof; I – top
of front step; J – front
of front step; K – side
of front step (cut out
two); L – top of back
step; M – front of back
step; N – side of back
step (cut out two).

F

G

H

I

L

J

K

M

N

Diagram 45 (continued) O – back/front of surplice (cut out two); P – sleeve of surplice (cut out two); Q – ruffle round neck; R – bow string (cut out two); S – bow itself (cut out two); T – book.

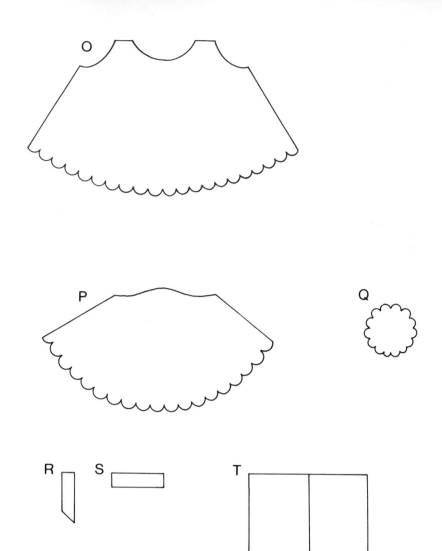

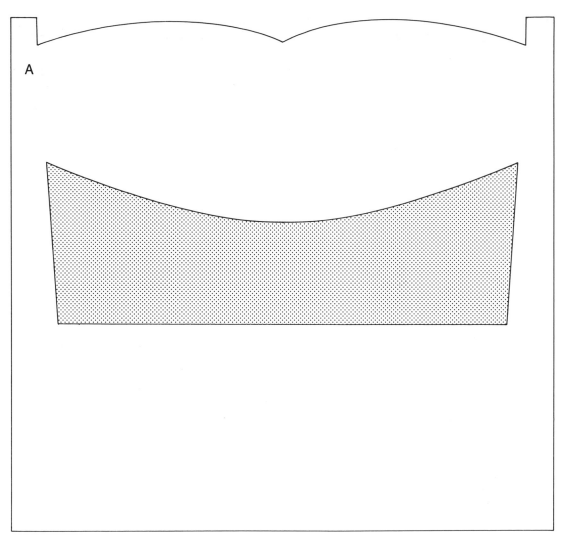

A

Diagram 46
Pattern pieces for cake
with teenager lounging
in his room (*plate 43*).
A – headboard (cut out
hatched section); B –
front of chest of
drawers (cut out
hatched section); C –
back of chest of
drawers.

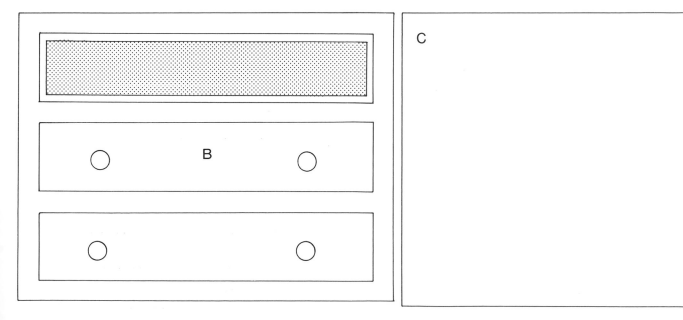

C

B

77

Diagram 46 (continued) D – side of chest of drawers (cut out two); E – top of chest of drawers; F – front of drawers (cut out three); G – base of drawer; H – back of drawer; I – side of drawer (cut out two); J – back of bedside cabinet; K – front of bedside cabinet; L – side of bedside cabinet (cut out two); M – top of bedside cabinet; N – front of bedside cabinet drawers (cut out three).

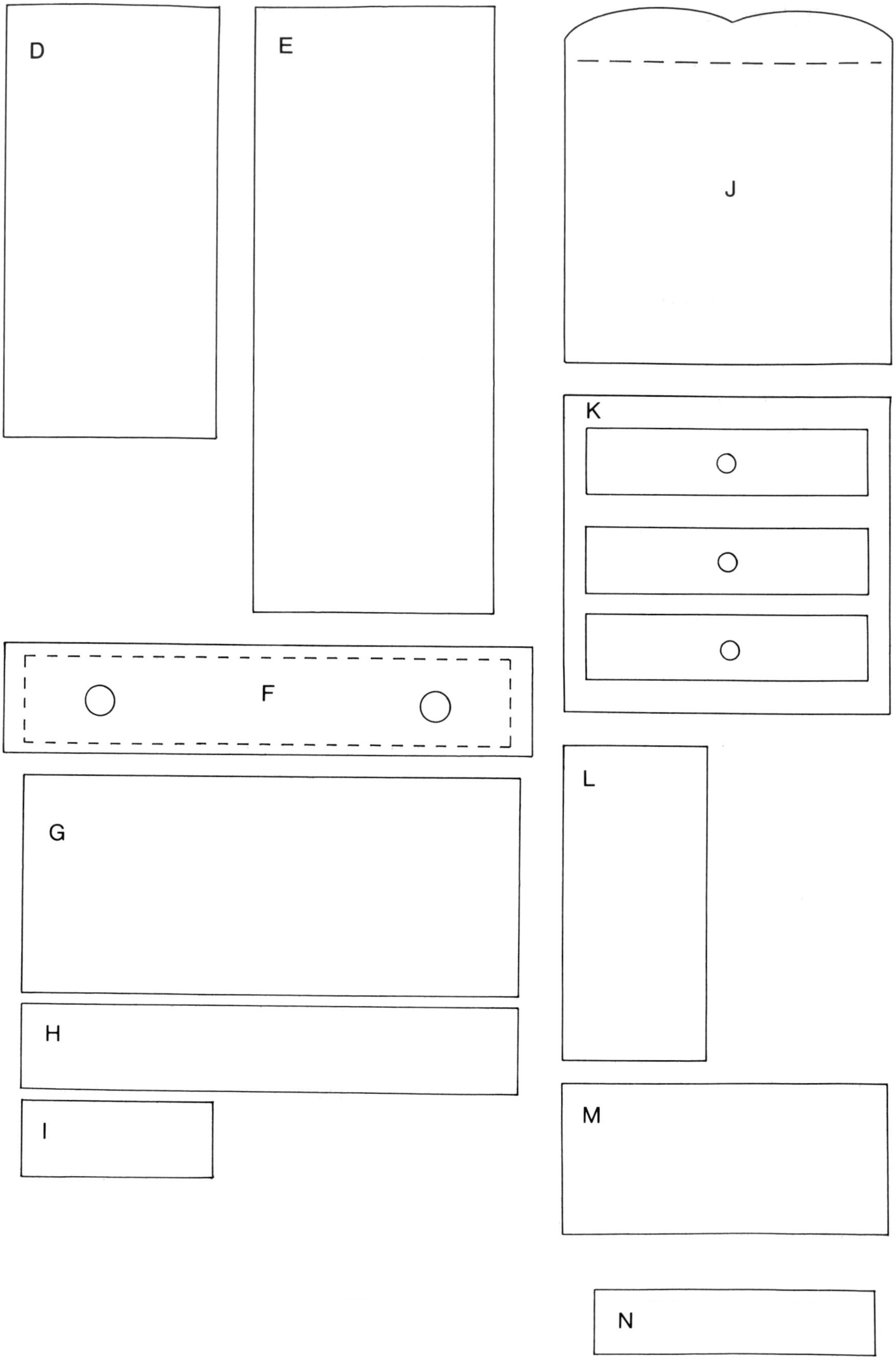

D

E

J

F

K

G

L

H

M

I

N

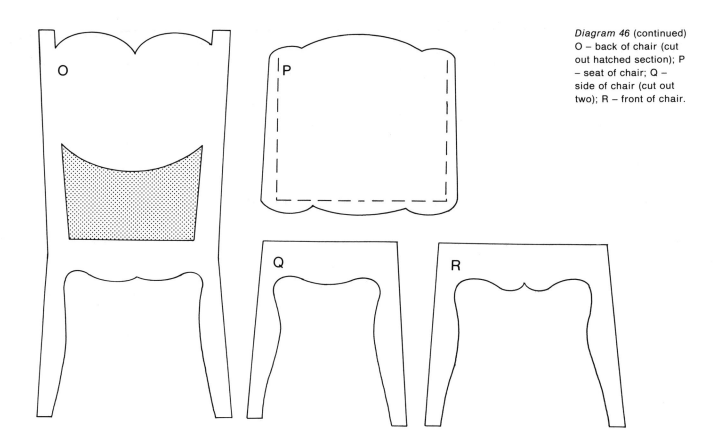

Diagram 46 (continued)
O – back of chair (cut
out hatched section); P
– seat of chair; Q –
side of chair (cut out
two); R – front of chair.

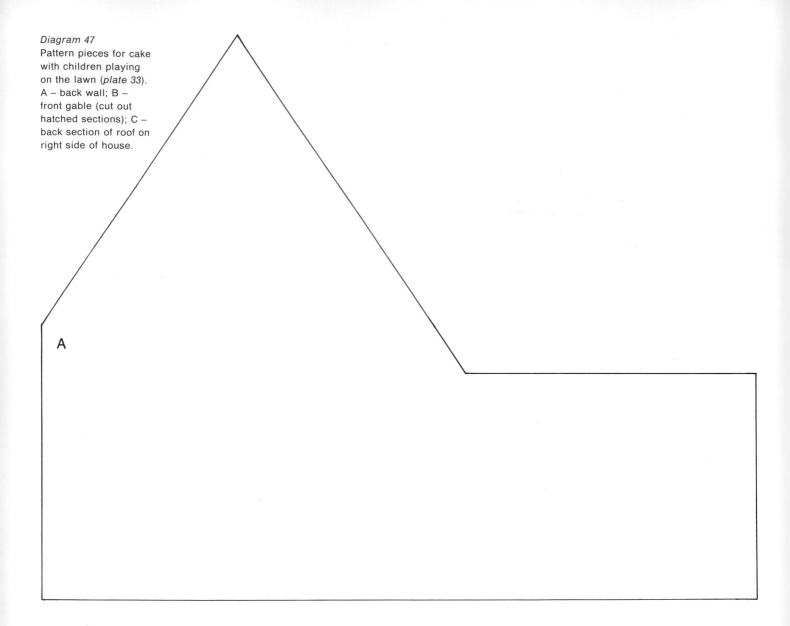

Diagram 47
Pattern pieces for cake
with children playing
on the lawn (*plate 33*).
A – back wall; B –
front gable (cut out
hatched sections); C –
back section of roof on
right side of house.

A

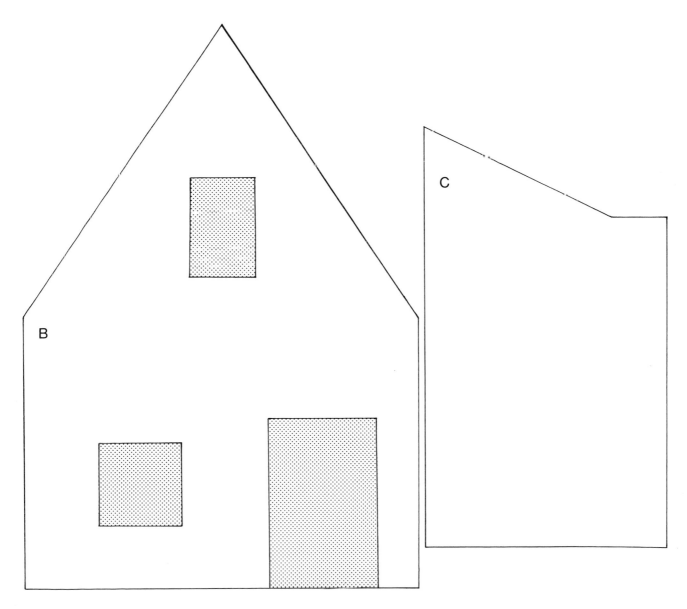

D – right front wall (cut out hatched section); E – side wall on right; F – side wall on left; G – front section of roof on right side of house; H – main roof on right side of house; I – main roof on left side of house.

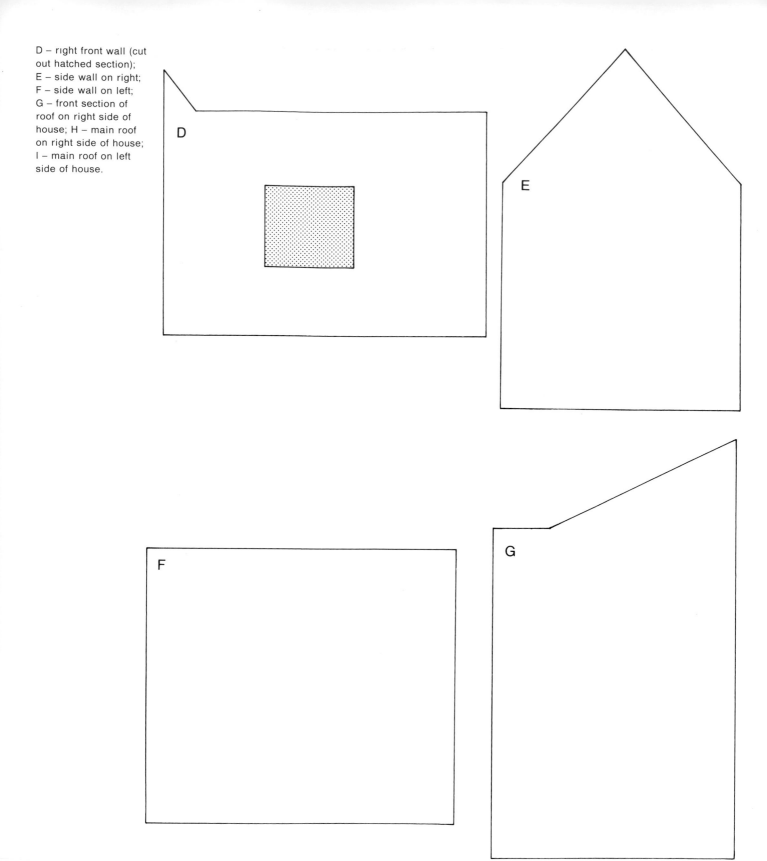

H

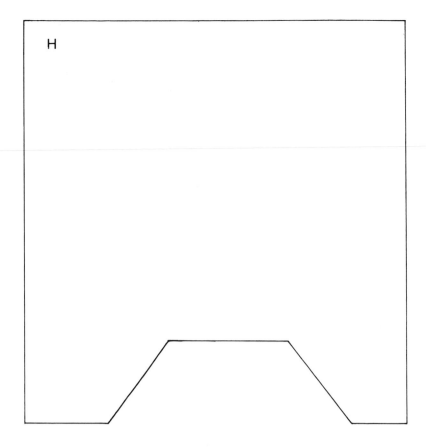

I

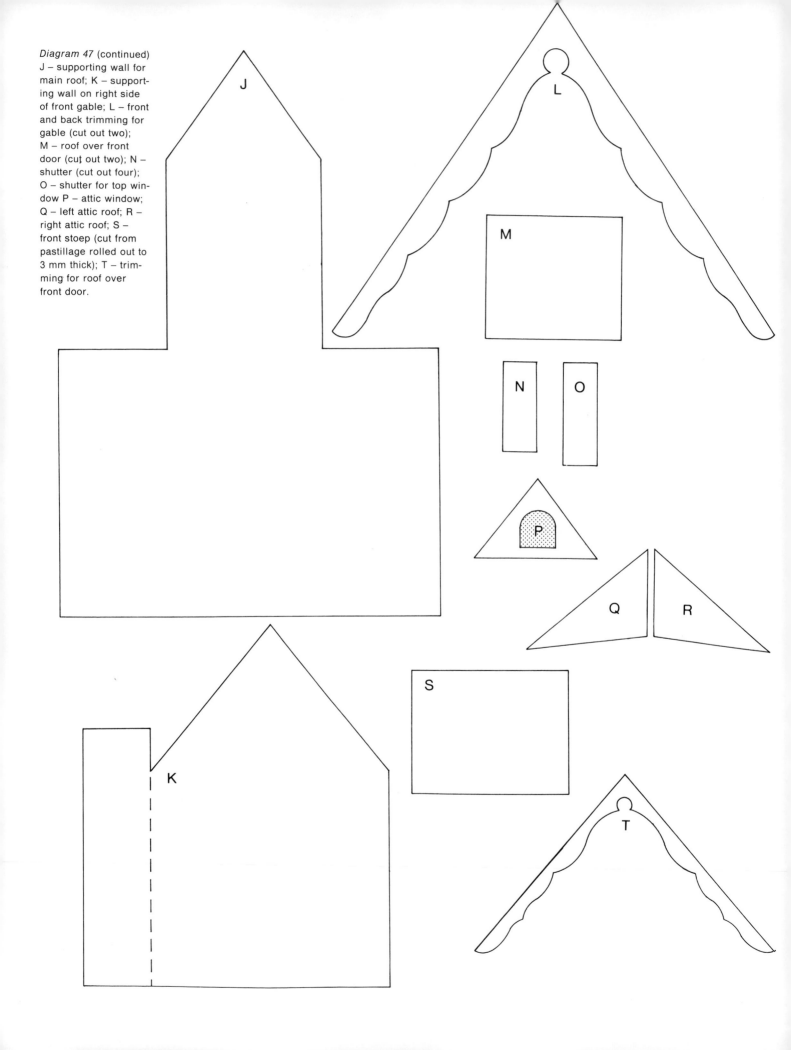

Diagram 47 (continued)
J – supporting wall for main roof; K – supporting wall on right side of front gable; L – front and back trimming for gable (cut out two); M – roof over front door (cut out two); N – shutter (cut out four); O – shutter for top window P – attic window; Q – left attic roof; R – right attic roof; S – front stoep (cut from pastillage rolled out to 3 mm thick); T – trimming for roof over front door.

Diagram 48
Embroidery pattern for
wedding cake with
purple wreath and
chrysanthemums
(*plate 11*).

Diagram 49
Embroidery pattern for
kidney-shaped wed-
ding cake in bas-relief
(*plate 16*).

85

Diagram 50
Embroidery pattern for
wedding cake with
bride and groom
(*plate 12*).

Diagram 51
Embroidery pattern for
two-tiered wedding
cake with blushing
brides (*plate 17*).

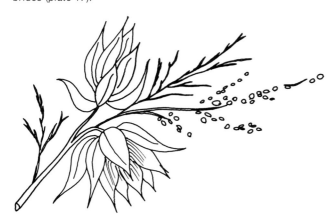
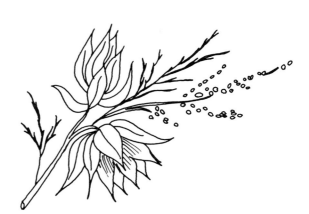

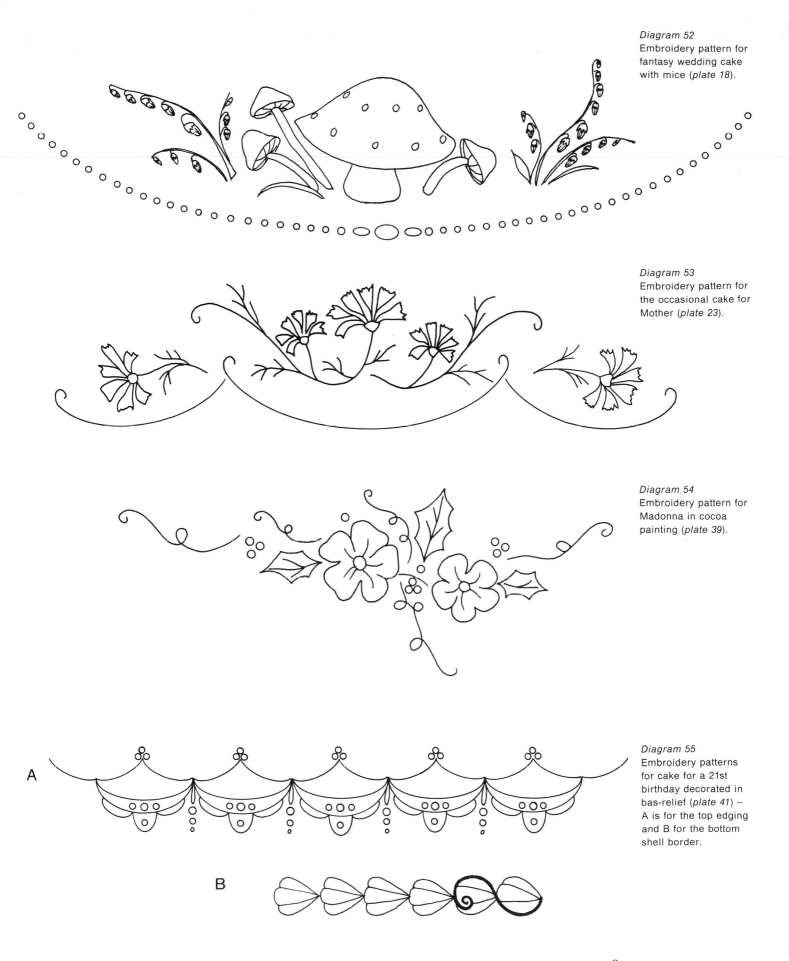

Diagram 52
Embroidery pattern for fantasy wedding cake with mice (*plate 18*).

Diagram 53
Embroidery pattern for the occasional cake for Mother (*plate 23*).

Diagram 54
Embroidery pattern for Madonna in cocoa painting (*plate 39*).

A

Diagram 55
Embroidery patterns for cake for a 21st birthday decorated in bas-relief (*plate 41*) – A is for the top edging and B for the bottom shell border.

B

Diagram 56
Embroidery pattern for cake for a girl's 21st birthday cake decorated with a picture in cocoa painting (*plate 45*).

Diagram 57
Embroidery pattern for board of a girl's 21st birthday decorated with a picture in cocoa painting (*plate 45*).

Diagram 58
Extra embroidery pattern.

Diagram 59
Extra embroidery
pattern.

Diagram 60
Extra embroidery
pattern.

Diagram 61
Shell and lace patterns. A – lace pattern for two-tiered wedding cake with blushing brides (*plate 17*); B – lace pattern for fantasy wedding or anniversary cake with mice (*plate 19*); H – lace pattern for the occasional cake for Mother (*plate 23*); I – lace pattern for kidney-shaped wedding cake in bas-relief (*plate 16*); J – lace pattern for wedding cake with purple wreath and chrysanthemums (*plate 11*). The rest of the patterns are extra.

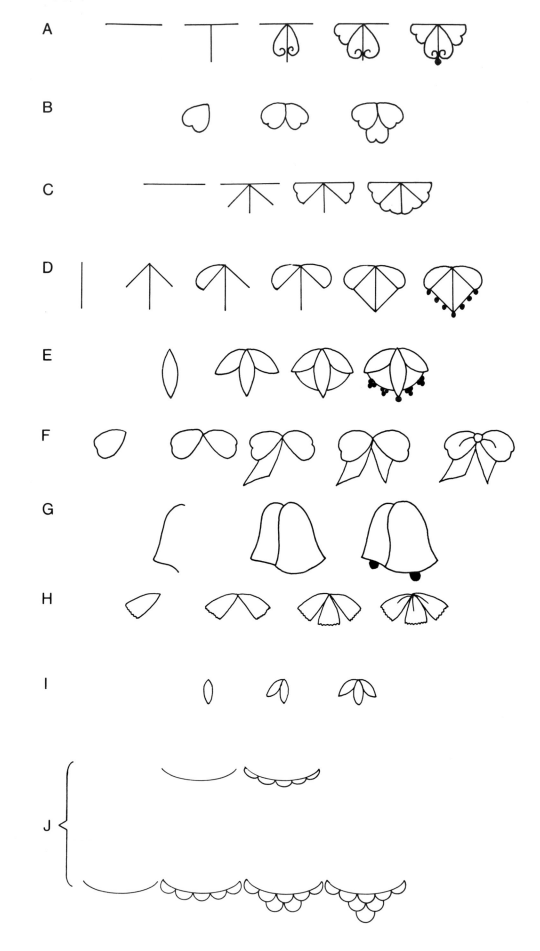